The World at 2000

Arabia without Sultans

Iran: Dictatorship and Development

Threat from the East? Soviet Policy in the Arc of Crisis

The Ethiopian Revolution (*co-author*)

The Making of the Second Cold War

State and Ideology in the Middle East and Pakistan (*co-editor*)

Cold War, Third World

Revolution and Foreign Policy: The Case of South Yemen, 1967–1987

Arabs in Exile: Yemeni Migrants in Urban Britain

Islam and the Myth of Confrontation: Religion and Politics in the Middle East

Rethinking International Relations

Revolution and World Politics: The Rise and Fall of the Sixth Great Power

Nation and Religion in the Middle East

The World at 2000

Perils and Promises

Fred Halliday

palgrave

First published 2001 by
PALGRAVE
Houndmills, Basingstoke, Hampshire RG21 6XS and
175 Fifth Avenue, New York, N. Y. 10010
Companies and representatives throughout the world

PALGRAVE is the new global academic imprint of
St. Martin's Press LLC Scholarly and Reference Division and
Palgrave Publishers Ltd (formerly Macmillan Press Ltd).

ISBN 0–333–94534–4 hardback
ISBN 0–333–94535–2 paperback

This book is printed on paper suitable for recycling and made from fully managed and sustained forest sources.

A catalogue record for this book is available from the British Library.

Library of Congress Cataloging-in-Publication Data

Halliday, Fred
The world at 2000–Perils and promises–Fred Halliday.
p.cm.
Includes bibliographical references and index.
ISBN 0–333–94534–4 – ISBN 0–333–94535–2 (pbk.)
1. World politics–21st century. 2. Globalization. 3. Democracy.
4. Security, International. I. Title: World at two-thousand.
II. Title.

D2003 .H35 2000
909.83–dc21   00–062604

Editing and origination by
Aardvark Editorial, Mendham, Suffolk
10   9   8   7   6   5   4   3   2   1
10   09 08 07 06 05 04 03 02 01

Printed and bound in Great Britain by
Creative Print & Design (Wales) Ebbw Vale

For Alex

Contents

Preface

The book that follows is based on a set of public lectures given at the London School of Economics in spring 2000: conceived of as part of the LSE's 'Spanning the Centuries' series, they were designed to explore broad themes in the field of international relations.

Throughout I have been aware of the pitfalls of such a speculative venture – the risks of any attempt to identify the major issues in world politics, the folly of prediction about human affairs, the particular dangers of verbosity that beset those who take as their starting point the millennium. That the very date 2000 is not, of course, of such import to those who have different calendars – be they Muslim, Iranian, Jewish, Ethiopian, or Japanese – is itself a corrective to any inflated privilege of global perspective: for them it is 1420, 1379, 5760, 1992 and 12 respectively.

The book is intended as a contribution to a number of key current academic and public debates about international relations, and hopefully one that will cross divisions of calendar and culture. While no reader will agree with everything in this book, it should be possible to conduct discussion of the issues it raises on the basis of facts and reasoning, and of some shared criteria. The realm of the international need not be conceded either to the emotional or the particularist, nor to the deterministic.

This book, therefore, rests on an argument for what I term 'international reason', this understood in two senses: analysing international relations in terms, analytic and moral, that aspire to being rational and universal, and assessing disputes within international relations through rational argument.

In preparing these lectures, and in reworking them for publication, I have also sought to strike a distinctive note, to avoid the two besetting vices of much writing on international affairs, complacency disguised as realism, and irresponsibility posing as conscience. In this vein, I try to chart a course that is both critical of the state of the contemporary world and exigent about that which may present itself as an alternative.

A number of people are owed a particular debt for their contribution to the completion of this book. My publisher Steven Kennedy both encouraged me to attempt these lectures and acted as a sympathetic editor throughout. *Radical Philosophy* kindly agreed to let me use material in Chapter 2, which was originally published in Issue 98, November–December 1999. The Foreign Policy Centre generously acted as co-sponsors of the lecture series. Amanda Goodall was enthusiastic in incorporating me into the LSE's 'Spanning the Centuries' programme. Gary Delaney, Sarah Smith and Clare Devaney of the LSE Conference and Events Office arranged the lectures themselves. Jennifer Chapa of the Department of International Relations LSE was invaluable in support for completion of lectures and book. Among those to whom I owe a particular intellectual gratitude I would mention Nuri Abd al-Razzaq, Mariano Aguirre, Fabian Biancardi, Nick Bisley, Tony Cole, Katerina Dalacoura, Wolfgang Deckers, Meghnad Desai, Edmund Fawcett, Graham Fuller, Tony Giddens, David Held, Christopher Hill, Dominique Jacquin-Berdal, Mary Kaldor, Gerison Lansdown, Margot Light, Jim Paul, Dennis Sammut, Jonathan Steele, Grahame Thompson and William Wallace. To my students over the years in the International Relations Department at LSE I owe stimulation and contestation. Finally, my family, Maxine and Alex, had to start the new millennium by putting up with more than the usual aberrant intensity that accompanies work of this kind. To all of them, for their patience and support, I give my heartfelt thanks and offer the excuse which goes for the book as a whole: it is only 2000 once.

FRED HALLIDAY
London
September 2000

List of Acronyms

ABM	anti-ballistic missile
AIDS	Acquired Immune Deficiency Syndrome
ANC	African National Congress
BINGO	business-supported international non-governmental organization
CNN	Cable News Network
CTBT	Comprehensive Test Ban Treaty
ELN	Ejercito de Liberación Nacional
EU	European Union
FARC	Fuerzas Armadas Revolucionarias de Colombia
FDI	foreign direct investment
FRETILIN	Revolutionary Front for an Independent East Timor
GDP	gross domestic product
GINGO	government-controlled international non-governmental organization
GM	genetically modified
ICANN	Internet Corporation for Assigned Names and Numbers
IMF	International Monetary Fund
INGO	international non-governmental organization
IRA	Irish Republican Army
KGB	Committee of State Security/(USSR state secret police)
KLA	Kosovo Liberation Army
MNC	multinational corporation
NAFTA	North American Free Trade Agreement
NATO	North Atlantic Treaty Organization
NGO	non-governmental organization
NIEO	New International Economic Order
NMD	National Missile Defense
NPT	Non-Proliferation Treaty
OAU	Organization for African Unity
OECD	Organization for Economic Cooperation and Development
OPEC	Organization of Petroleum Exporting Countries

OSCE	Organization for Security and Cooperation in Europe
PKK	*Partiya Karkeran Kurdistan* (Kurdistan Workers' Party)
PLO	Palestine Liberation Organization
RINGO	reactionary international non-governmental organization
RMA	revolution in military affairs
TINGO	tribal international non-governmental organization
UN	United Nations
UNDP	United Nations Development Programme
WMD	weapons of mass destruction
WTO	World Trade Organization

1

A World in Transition

On 1 January 2000 a world of just over 6 billion people, divided into 195 different states, with up to 10,000 spoken languages, entered a new millennium. Contrary to the fears of many, there were no midnight catastrophes, no breakdowns of technology, no religious or political upheavals, no apocalyptic strikes of nature. After a century of major wars, most of the world was at peace, but not all – about two dozen wars raged and in the months preceding 1 January both major powers in the world had themselves been at war, the USA in Kosovo, the Russians in Chechnya. Whatever else divided them, the world's 3 billion labour force was united in one common endeavour, that of seeking to find and retain a source of income.

The onset of a new epoch, however arbitrarily defined, is a time for stocktaking and, as befits such a moment, for a note of reason and of optimism. 'A Revolution in Human Affairs. An Intense Sense of Change Grips Much of the World' proclaimed the *International Herald Tribune* in its issue of Monday, 3 January 2000. There are, broadly put, five good reasons for being optimistic, and more optimistic than in earlier times, about the course of the international system. First of all, since the end of the cold war in 1991, the world no longer lives under the shadow of a global strategic rivalry, one that brought with it the danger of the nuclear annihilation of humanity. That is no small advance, and one which, for the foreseeable future, we can remain thankful. The great French writer Raymond Aron summed up the cold war and its arms race in the words *paix impossible, guerre improbable*.[1] We have now moved to a state of *paix improbable, guerre improbable*, which is a significant shade better. Second, states have, over recent decades, developed a widespread network of co-operation, most evident in the European Union (EU) but reflected in a complex set of governance institutions. The international system has shed part of its anarchic,

1

competitive character. Third, we live in an era of unprecedented economic growth: over the past 50 years, global GDP has increased ninefold, from $3 trillion to $30 trillion, average per capita incomes have risen more than three times, and the percentage of the world enjoying what is termed 'medium human development' has risen from 55% to 66%. There is good reason, moreover, to expect that these levels of growth in world GDP and in the diffusion of part of that wealth will continue. This economic growth has been accompanied by the formation of powerful new trading areas, with political concomitants, of which the EU, a unique and far from preordained success, is the most striking example. Fourth, despite the claims of nationalists, clergymen and some political philosophers, we no longer live in a world riven by fundamental ideological division, or, equally important, in one of incommensurable or non-communicable value differences. There is plenty of variety and dispute in the world, for the sound reason that traditions and interests vary: but this division is framed, and argued out, in terms that are to a considerable degree shared – independence, popular and national sovereignty, rights, economic prosperity. There is a common global ethical language: the dispute is what to say in it. Arguments about global injustice, double standards and inequality at least imply that there are universal criteria for arguing about these. Every contestant can find support for their claims in the UN Charter. Finally, we see no end to the advance of science and technology. There is enormous, and justified, concern about how this knowledge will be distributed. But the ability of science to enhance our lives, and our bodies and health, holds out enormous potential for humanity as a whole. Increases in lifespan are evident around the world and dramatic new developments are on the way: the twenty-first century promises, if nothing else, to be the age of biology. Indeed, the most dramatic news of the new millennium came on 26 June 2000, when the mapping of the 3.5 billion components of the human genetic structure was announced.

So much for the good news, or the potential for good news. To turn now to the challenges this situation poses. It is necessary, especially at a time of widespread complacency, to strike a note of warning: the last century began for many in 1900 on a note of optimism and progress, *la belle époque*, only to founder within a decade and a half in 1914. We would be wise to recall such a confounding of human expectations: the next century could turn out to be better than that which has passed, but it could turn out to be as bad, or worse.[2] We live, above all, in a time of historic indeterminacy.

Although there has been no shortage of contenders, the present period of international relations, irrespective of the millennium, is one that is remarkably hard to define: there is no 'New World Order'; we cannot call it 'the Interregnum' until we know what it is an interregnum between; the 'Clash of Civilizations' sounds good to some, but lacks empirical or analytic rigour; despite the claims of some this is not a 'World Without Meaning' as those many who seek to make money would be quick to assert; the 'New Middle Ages' would sound rather odd to anyone who had lived through the real medieval period. We do not yet have a shape for the post-cold-war world, the pattern of great power relations is in many ways in flux, the world economy occasions many uncertainties. The only epochal cliché *not* used is 'crisis.'

The reasons for optimism may be easily offset by those for pessimism. On present form, the world will be lucky to get through the next 25 years without a nuclear exchange between regional rivals. Inequalities of power between states and peoples are increasing. A range of destructive forces – inter-ethnic conflicts, economic inequalities, the spread of illegal trade in drugs and weapons – are growing. The last century saw much abuse of science, by states, and the next one promises to see more abuse, by private interests, especially in biotechnology. Humanity, all six billion of us, is to a greater or lesser extent in forms of denial about what is happening to the environment, and in the field of public health, above all with regard to AIDS and the return of previously eradicated illnesses.

To the uncertainty of these trends can be added our very uncertainty about what to look at. The French *Annales* school of historians famously distinguished between three time-scales within which to view events – the secular or *longue durée*, the immediate or *événementiel* and the intermediate or *conjoncturel*: the immediate is not to be discounted, especially if it involves wars, revolutions or economic crises, and the secular may be too long to evaluate except in retrospect. Yet much of the debate we can have is not about what is happening in the immediate, but about which conjunctural trends may be more significant: October 1999 was a good challenge to any such approach. This was the month in which we saw two of the most ominous developments in recent international political life and ones which, by the time the world gets to 2050, could be of decisive importance. October 1999 was the month of the US Senate's rejection of the Comprehensive Test Ban Treaty (CTBT). It was also, as Eric Hobsbawm emphasized in his own millennial work, the month in which the world's population passed the 6 billion mark.[3] The former occurred on 14 October, the latter was deemed by the UN to have taken place on 12 October. The question of how these events – degradation in the world's inter-state security situation and demographic explosion – will interact in the mid-term, over some decades, as well as what they portend, goes to the heart of analysing international relations.

Against this background it is possible to look in more detail at some of the challenges faced in discussion of the contemporary international system. These can be divided into two groups – the historic and the intellectual. An argument for international reason and a measured if reserved optimism presuppose not only that we can talk meaningfully about the issues of historical development, but that our discussion of the second group of challenges, the intellectual, could bear some relevance to the first. This is indeed part of the test of an international reason.

Movements of History

Amidst the many broad questions that may be asked about the direction of the world at the start of the new millennium, there are at least four which command particular attention.

Geographic shifts

For five hundred years the centre of global economic and military power has lain in the northern Atlantic, divided between the major states of Europe and the eastern seaboard of the USA. Slowly, but it seems inexorably, this is beginning to change. The rise of East Asian powers, first Japan and now a broader range of states, most importantly the growing economic strength of China, combined with the shift in US attention from the Atlantic to the Pacific, indicate that a tectonic shift may be under way. This is not a 'decline of the west' as so long presaged in conservative European thought, not least because it rests in part on prosperity along the US Pacific coast. The signs of this are evident – in commercial and political terms. The East Asian region accounts for an increasingly higher percentage of world GDP. This shift from the Atlantic to the Pacific is compounded by a shift within the USA itself. It is Silicon Valley in California, not the industrial heartlands of the north-east, which is the centre of the American economic advance associated with computerization. In the military field, it is to East Asia that the USA increasingly directs its concerns.

The question marks over this process remain enormous. Japan in the 1990s experienced prolonged stagnation. The Chinese economic boom could founder in social and political chaos. The East Asian currency crisis of 1997 demonstrated underlying weaknesses in markets and government structure. For its part, Europe, with an economically viable Union and growing competitiveness in the world economy, may be able to reassert itself against its major competitors in the USA and Asia. We are also far from the world of discrete, competitive trading blocs and empires of the early twentieth century. A prosperous world economy, and free movement of goods and capital, is one that would make the East Asian and European expansions compatible and mutually reinforcing. The economic values which are being espoused in Asia are, to a considerable degree, ones derived from, and similar to, those of Europe. Yet an epoch of European and Atlantic domination, which spanned the different phases of subjugation of the non-European world, and of empires, informal and formal, does appear to be waning.

The nature of power

In the international domain power has three main forms – military, economic, and cultural or ideological. Traditionally, power in the international arena rested on military power. On its own this was never sufficient, since military capability presupposed economic capability and the political cohesion of the state in question. Moreover, while military power was the most important form of power, it was not necessarily the main motive for the expansion of state interests: the expansion of European states across the world, from the late-fifteenth century onwards, was secured by military means but driven in large measure by the desire for profit and materials. The domination of the world by modern empires, notably in the colonial period, enmeshed military with economic and cultural power.

In the contemporary world this predominance of military power may, in some degree, be eroding. First, the invention of nuclear weapons in the 1940s has made war between major states not impossible, but most unlikely. Second, the power of states has come more and more to be separate from territorial control and to rest on economic power, in the form of investment and commercial strength, and on forms of culture: technology, involving both economic and cultural dimensions, has confirmed this shift away from military power. The influence of the USA in the fields of satellite media, cinema, popular music and the English language itself all confirm this development of what are termed 'soft' forms of power. How far this is going is, however, another question. The ability to project economic and cultural power rests to a considerable degree on military capacity – or, as in the case of Germany and Japan, on the willingness of another power, in this case the USA, to protect them.

Much is made of the twin defeats of the great powers of the cold war in Third World conflicts with much weaker enemies – of the Americans in Vietnam and the Russians in Afghanistan. But these conflicts did not in themselves demonstrate the obsolescence of military power: the Vietnamese were armed by Russia and China, the Afghan guerrillas by the USA. These wars were both followed by conflicts in which military power was used to traditional effect, to defeat rival states – in Kuwait in 1991, and in Kosovo in 1999. The US concern in the new international context, to increase its military dominance, especially through the use of precision-guided weapons and intelligence superiority, the 'Revolution in Military Affairs', does not suggest the end of military power. The relation between the three forms of power may be changing, the dependence of each on the other is not. More serious may be the limits on the state or any other form of power posed by new cross-border challenges: illegal movement of peoples, transnational crime, environmental degradation, narcotics, disease. Here classical state-centred solutions are not available. Yet if there is to be a solution or coherent policy response, it is with the state that these must start.

The role of the state

Central to discussion of underlying trends in the world today is analysis of the power of states and the degree to which their powers are changing, or being eroded. States, understood not as communities of peoples but as institutions, as centres of coercive and administrative power and as objects of legitimacy, have existed for thousands of years. But the modern state, with its particular extensive powers, and claim to democratic and national legitimacy, is a product of the past two centuries. It is over this time, concomitant with the Industrial Revolution and the transformation of domestic society, that the state as we know it has been created. Until recently it has appeared as if the power of the state has grown stronger: in particular the power of the state to control the transfer of goods, ideas and people across frontiers has grown. Recently, however, it has appeared as if the powers of the state are declining – a result of privatization and neo-liberal thinking within, and of an erosion of state control of cross-frontier activities without. The Keynesian model of economic management, prevalent in western Europe after 1945, began to erode in the 1970s. Communism was the last attempt of modern times by a group of states to control what moved across their frontiers, and, not least, prevent their own people from crossing those borders. The widely debated phenomenon of globalization (see Chapter 5) is closely associated with a declining role of the state, as movements of capital, goods and ideas escape the control of governments.

It is far too simple, however, to argue that in the developed world the state is losing its power in any overall sense. Globalization does reduce the ability of individual states to control the movements of goods and capital across frontiers. Equally it lessens the control of ideas. The attempt to regulate the movements of people, within or without a just legal regime, is proving elusive. Yet in certain other respects the state retains its central role. It remains a dominant factor in the economy of all OECD states, accounting for, on average, 40% of GDP. It retains a security role: the maintenance of order within states, and in the air and sea outside of them, is a precondition for the very process of globalization itself. The international institutions, notably the EU, that have been constructed between some states rest on the support – political, financial, economic – of their individual state members: they are far from being independent of states in any meaningful sense. States continue within their own domains to regulate trade and finance, and to enforce law. At the same time, states remain the focus for the political commitments that underlie the whole of the contemporary world. Where democracy prevails, it is first and foremost democracy within that particular state that is the basis for political life. Whether or not democracy prevails, the state remains the focus of national identification for most of those who live under it. Beyond the developed world the picture is, in part, different. Here the economic and coercive powers of the state may be weaker, its claims on popular support more tenuous. Yet this is far from being the norm. In the industrializing states of East Asia it has been the very interventions of the state – in education, banking, investment – that have spurred economic development. In Arab and African states strong coercive regimes have remained. The prevalence of nationalism in democratic and authoritarian states is testimony to the continued belief of most of humanity in the legitimacy of states, and if not the state they live in, then the one they would like to live in.

A *changing map: secession and fusion*

A question acutely posed by the survival of states is that of their cohesion. The map of around 195 states in the world is arbitrary, and often contested. It corresponds in only the weakest manner to existing groups of linguistic or other peoples. Even those states which appear to be the most coherent and historically based have come about through conquest, forced cultural homogenization and the denial of diversity and pre-existing transnational linkages. Yet it is this map which forms the basis of a world political order, of the growth of democratic politics and of legitimacy and sentiment.

This map was the result of two historical forces above all – in the case of Europe, war, and elsewhere imperialism. Indeed imperialism, far from dividing, had forged new entities: countries as diverse as Ireland and India were formed into single political units by colonialism, others, across Africa, Australasia and the Americas, were invented in the imperial epoch. In the period of the cold war there were many attempts to redraw the map: former colonies became independent more or less within the frontiers of the colonial entities themselves, but in the main the map held. There was only one case of secession, that of Bangladesh from Pakistan in 1971. Some entities that might have attained independence failed to do so because they were occupied at the moment of independence by enemies – Palestine by Israel and Jordan in 1948–49, Tibet by China in 1950, Sahara by Morocco in 1975, East Timor by Indonesia in 1975. The end of the cold war, however, led to the breakup of four multi-ethnic states – the

USSR, Czechoslovakia, Yugoslavia, Ethiopia. Over twenty new independent states emerged. Elsewhere – in Spain, parts of Latin America and the Middle East, India – there was renewed interest in secession. The question was how far would it go. Some speculated that as part of the crisis of the state worldwide we could see hundreds of new states emerging, perhaps small and beautiful, perhaps not.[4]

Widespread fragmentation would, indeed, mark a major shift in the world. Yet the breakup of states may be a less significant trend than appeared in the first flush of post-communist secession. First, the crisis of authority that led to the post-communist secessions was largely specific to the communist states: elsewhere the regimes were not willing to let their regions go nor was the international community so quick to encourage this. The Kurds, after the independence of Ukraine the largest community without a state, did not benefit from the end of communism. Second, where independence did become possible – Namibia, Palestine, East Timor and at some point in the future West Caledonia – this was very much the tail end of decolonization. Most importantly of all, however, the major trend in the international arena as far as redrawing the map was concerned was not secession, but fusion, again in cases where the end of the cold war opened up new possibilities. The reunification of Germany in 1990 was the most decisive event for Europe since 1945, not the independence of Slovenia, Moldova or Georgia. In the Middle East the only case of a unification of Arab states that was sustained, with some significant coercion by the stronger North, was that of the two Yemens, commenced in 1990, sealed in a civil war in 1994. In East Asia the unification of the two Koreas is, sooner or later, a high probability. Above all, the unification of the three Chinas – Beijing, Hong Kong, Taipei – is the dominant question of the coming years. It is this process of unification of states, not their secession, which is, combined with broader forms of regional integration, the most challenging feature of changes in the contemporary world map.

Intellectual Challenges

Interdependence

Central to analysing the contemporary world is the question of how we understand the impact on our everyday lives, and on our societies, of the international. To an unprecedented degree, people today in every country are conscious of the multifarious ways in which their lives are affected by what goes on beyond the frontiers of their own state. We live in an increasingly interactive world, not only in regard to the world economy, or the global environment, or the spread of new political ideas, but also in regard to food, music, clothes, gender roles, health and, not least, the forms and changing forms of communication. This is evident in the very definition of the good life and what people, especially young people, aspire to. It is equally evident in the threats people face, or imagine they face.

Some forms of caution are, however, in order here. First we should not exaggerate the degree to which the world really is united, a global village, 'wired' or whatever: on any index you take, be it food, investment or language, the world remains a diverse and, to a considerable degree, fragmented place. This is true for historic reasons but also because globalization itself encourages, or provokes, new forms of diversity – in music, dress, food and above all sentiment. The spread of globalization in terms of growth, trade, investment, and life chances is also very selective. There is room too for disagreement about the novelty of this interconnectedness: it is a conceit of the more developed and hitherto insulated countries that this interconnection is a recent development. In the USA and Europe writers began in the 1970s and 80s to discover something called 'interdependence'. By this they meant the vulnerability of one society to events in another – the OPEC oil price rises of 1971–73 or the Vietnam War. But this was very much an illusion of the few, very few, societies that had not been affected, buffeted, if not ravaged, by colonialism and the politics of the nineteenth and twentieth centuries: for over 90% of the world, indeed for all but perhaps the UK, Sweden, Canada and the USA this experience of vulnerability was not new. Even they, as shown by the experience of the crash of 1929 and two world wars, had not been as insulated as people thought. Third, this emphasis on external influence does not entail determination: we are not in any society passive objects of global trends, but can, to a considerable degree, choose responses to them. How this happens – what limits on choice, but also what increases of choice, are created by contemporary trends – is a central question of our time.

Insecurity

One of the topics most discussed in social science today, and in business, is risk. It is generally held that in certain crucial respects risk has in recent decades increased, be it in regard to health, to financial calculation or to the physical security of the individual. For the individual walking the streets of a major city at night the risks may be more to person, from society, than from the threat posed by another state, or by opponents of one's own state. Each social science plies its wares in this field – economics, sociology, psychology and accountancy. However, the greatest risks are arguably the ones dealt with in international relations, and have been so for some decades. These include the risks of miscalculation amidst foreign policy crises, the risk involved in intervening, or not intervening, in the domestic conflicts of other states, above all the lingering risk of nuclear war.

These are the classic, long recognized forms of insecurity involved in international relations. The range of insecurities is, however, changing: to these dramatic, classical forms of risk we can add others – the risks involved in not addressing the long-term decay of the global environment, or in allowing the gap between rich and poor to increase every decade, the risks posed by the spread of AIDS and the resurgence of previously contained public health dangers, the risks posed by new forms of transnational criminal activity, in regard to drugs, kidnapping of women, the spread of small arms. A heroin processing plant in Colombia or Afghanistan, an environmental degradation in the tropics, a refugee crisis in the Balkans, a banking collapse in South-east Asia all raise issues of security that affect people thousands of miles away. This partial redefinition of insecurity is compounded by changes in communications: the greater ease with which people, goods *and* information are moved around the world. Indeed one of the fastest growing areas of concern with security lies in the vulnerability of global information circuits to unauthorized access or attack.

The argument for informed rational discussion of international relations is in part based on this very issue, on the dangers posed to security in the international sphere: herein lies the fallacy of ignoring that which lies beyond the frontiers of one's own state, epitomized in the retreat of the media in most developed countries into what are termed 'domestic' or 'family interest' programmes. At the same time, the question arises of *how* these different forms of insecurity interact. A connection between economic insecurity and war has long been evident, be it in the quest for resources and control of trading routes to the impact, conjunctural indeed, of the great depression of 1929 on the politics of Europe. Economic insecurity and competition retain their ability to promote conflict, as is evident in the Persian Gulf and in East Asia. Less clear, but potentially ominous, is the impact on security traditionally defined of developments in the drugs trade, the spread of AIDS or conflict over environmental policies. When it comes to the challenge of malevolent hackers, or freelance promoters of biological warfare, it is harder still to calibrate the risk. At the same time, as in matters of military insecurity, there are many who, for reasons intellectual or financial, have an interest in exaggerating the risk. Intellectual abnegation, and political and media avoidance on one side, alarmist threat exaggeration on the other, can only heighten the longer-run impact of these uncertainties.

Global mythologies

Every intellectual field involves engagement with some form of distortion, misrepresentation, myth, irrationality: it is one of the functions of an academic discipline to identify, and counter, such myths. Globalization produces greater contact between people but it may also produce greater misunderstanding. A key intellectual challenge of the world at 2000 relates to the myth, distortion and misuse of historical explanation and example which are encountered in discussion of the international system. This, it can be argued, is one of the least studied aspects of globalization – a trend to paranoia and conspiracy theory that was promoted first by colonialism, then given a new lease of life by the cold war, and has now reached its current, globally wired culmination. Paranoia, not a single financial market, is arguably the highest stage of globalization.

It was Francis Bacon who in his *Novum Organum* (1620) introduced a scientific approach by arguing against the various 'Idols' that beset the minds of men and women. In this regard international relations is no laggard. One has only to look at the press of any country or at the speeches of politicians, or to catch what attitudes are expressed in everyday contexts, to realize what a mass of prejudice and myth prevails about matters international. Western Europeans may like to think that it is others – Serbs worried about the Turks, Chinese enraged about the bombing of their Belgrade embassy, Muslims concerned with western 'plots' – who think in terms of conspiracy. But this is far from being the case. We need only listen or read what significant portions of the British press have to say about Brussels. We can look at what much of the European left thinks about the USA or what many in the USA think about the UN or international adjudications that go against them. There is no need to loiter on speculation concerning the death of Princess Diana, the crash off New York of TWA 800, or the death of President Kennedy. To these myths of conspiracy there are those of national enmity and simplification: the British press, and increasingly the TV, replicate these happily about Germans, French, Muslims and the like. It is one of the paradoxes of globalization that it produces a context for greater mythology about the international even as it promises a media that are more and more parochial in interest. Among democratic countries, the British press are strong contenders for the gold medal in this regard.

In terms of ethnocentric bigotry, we truly live in a globalized world. Such mythology, like so much other ideology, is loudmouthed about its distinctiveness, yet similar, indeed, modular, in form: every nation thinks it is the most put upon. Education, travel, modernity itself may lessen this, but can also make it worse: arms manufacturers control American foreign policy, the British are always scheming against one or other people, the Americans are always throwing their weight around – these are among the more light-hearted of such myths. A visit to the Middle East, or South Asia, would give much more virulent and dangerous messages. Anyone who has followed the politics of the Balkans in the past ten years will find more than enough here, some of it too eagerly replicated by supposedly emphatic and partisan foreign observers. It is part of every nationalist ideology to create some apparently all-pervasive international conspiracy directed against their people: every event is part of a plot. Indeed the combination of transnational contact – think only of mass tourism – with an increasingly debased, sensationalized, and – the word is used advisedly – decadent press means that in many ways international understanding is declining. It can be argued that the degree of prejudice, the force of the 'idols' of the international, is greater than in any other domain of social activity.

Ethical choices

All of this leads to what is, arguably, the most important reason of all for analysing the international and never more so than at the present time, the nature of the policy choices involved and the moral issues these choices raise. As with risk, and idols of the mind, choice is certainly something that pervades all areas of human activity. But those choices pertaining to the international are, arguably, also of immense proportion: this applies to debates on such questions as war, migration, the world economy, the environment, human rights, to name but a few. Yet the weight of these issues contrasts with an almost wholly impoverished, and, again, simplified landscape of public debate. Everyone has strong views about morality in international affairs. 'Something has to be done' is a universal call, with the underlying premise that there is always something effective that can be done. Everyone is quick to justify their own side, with various forms of self-righteousness, itself both distinctive and modular, and to denounce everyone else. If there is one assumption which pervades much of the public debate in all countries, it tends to be that there *is* a simple answer: most people are sure, more sure than in most domestic disputes, that there is one right answer, their own, and that anyone who disagrees is a fool, a hypocrite, a knave, the tool of special interests, or just doing whatever they are doing to distract attention from domestic problems.

In moral discussion about international issues, you are not normally permitted much room for doubt, or for cautious exploration of different positions. Moral indignation may be out of fashion in domestic affairs, in class conflict, or inter-regional conflict, but in international affairs it is alive and well. Witness what were arguably the most important ethical disputes of the post-cold-war epoch, those over international intervention in the 1990s – over Kuwait in 1990–91, Bosnia in 1995, Kosovo in 1999. Look further at the clamour over such inter-ethnic conflicts as Chechnya, Palestine, Kurdistan, Kashmir, Tibet and East Timor. Again, it should not be thought that progress, modernity or globalization have brought such ethical choices to a consensual, globally convenient, end. If anything, the challenges of globalization make the arguments sharper: about migration, environmental burden-sharing, humanitarian intervention, the adjudication of trade disputes. Indignation and accusations of conspiracy and perfidy run high, evenness of argument, let alone a dose of self-awareness and self-criticism, run rather low. In many contexts ethical debate on international relations resembles nothing so much as that ultimate zero-sum contest, the football match.

Limits of the New

The challenges, historical and ethical, raised by the contemporary world, pose the question of evaluating how new the world of today actually is. There are two very common, and boring, responses to any contemporary situation. One is to say that 'nothing has changed'. At the root of this may, often do, lie certain general views about inherent human nature: leaders cannot be trusted, peoples are fickle and prone to extremes. In politics states and nations are still with us, old suspicions between peoples subsist and revive, the problems of the modern world – migration, proliferation, oil prices, religious fundamentalism – have all been with us before. 'Pull up the blankets, we can all go back to sleep' is the response. A more sophisticated variant of this is to say that everything we need to know is in the classics – Thucydides or Hobbes, Macchiavelli or, indeed, Marx. The classics and the history of past centuries do repay study: there is often more there than current fashion and enthusiasm would suggest. The same goes for literature. One of the best books on Saddam Hussein was written in 1591: *Richard III* by William Shakespeare.

It is impossible to read a passage from one of the great books of literature, or a poem written centuries ago, and not be struck by the contemporary relevance of what is written. In politics and international affairs people often like to add authority, and solemnity, to what they say about the present by a judicious invocation of the past: a generation ago, this would have been some reference to the Roman Empire or the Greek orators, today it is more likely to be some statement based on sociobiology or tribal behaviour; everyone, it seems now has a view on the dark ages. Yet this is nonetheless an insufficient answer. Human knowledge, scientific or literary, does develop, if only because the world it is describing is different. Industrialization, nuclear weapons, advances in medicine do alter the character of human relations, and of international relations. Few 50 years ago could have envisaged what the growth of the EU, or of nuclear weapons, could do to relations between states.

At the other end of the spectrum is the claim that everything is new. We live, we are sometimes told, in a world that has been transformed by something: sometimes it is a particular human catastrophe – Auschwitz, Sabra and Shatila, Srebrenica and Sarajevo – sometimes it is a social process – modernity, post-communism, the personal computer. Yet the claim of epochal novelty is itself old: religions, and revolutions, used, of course, to claim this in the past. In international relations and in the study of what is a composite process, globalization, we have no shortage of such claims: that distance, or nationality, or states have been dissolved. Great claims are currently being made for advances in two areas of human research – IT and biology. Yet here too some historical perspective may be in order. Migration has been a feature of world politics for hundreds of years. Religious ideas, and other destabilizing ideologies, have crossed frontiers for just as long – indeed arguably they were there before frontiers themselves. Jesus Christ, Buddha, the prophet Mohammed and Martin Luther would all be surprised to hear that the transnational flow of ideas is somehow a product of contemporary times.

The problem with many analyses of the contemporary world, and of the globalized, 'post-modern' or transnational character of these times, is not that what is claimed is false, but that it is not anything like as novel as its proponents claim it is. As will be discussed in Chapter 8, much is made these days about the role of culture in relations between peoples and in systems of power: it would come as a surprise to the Catholic Church, or to the proponents of the British Empire, that it should be any different. The challenge to us, the secret of contemporary analysis in any period indeed, is to avoid these two pitfalls: the world is neither wholly static nor wholly new. Somewhere in between, and in a manner itself always changing, lies our answer, 'our' in the sense that it is the answer that will give us the greatest ability to understand and control events, between the *événementiel* and the conjunctural.

So much for speculation about historical trends. The most important lesson of all from the past century is the ability of human affairs to surprise. Since 1990 we have seen the end of the cold war, the collapse of communism, the breakup of the USSR. It is true that there were those who foresaw this – but generally in a very different form from what actually happened. Contrary to much of what was later written, communism did not collapse because of revolt from below, let alone a revolt of the nationalities. It collapsed because of a loss of purpose and will at the top: dissent from below there most certainly was, but it acted, and came onto the streets, once the power and authority, and menace, of the state had receded. A second change has been that of globalization, a multifaceted process to which we will return. Both of these might appear to point in a salutary, even Whiggish, direction of growing espousal of liberal values. But other trends do not fit so easily into an optimistic liberal view of human progress. One of the most widely accepted accompaniments of modernity was secularization, not atheism in the sense of rejection of belief in God, but a gradual retreat of religious discourse and claims of religious authority from public life. Events in a range of countries – not just some, a minority, to be sure, of Muslim states, but in India, Israel and the United States – appear to counter this trend. China, in which it was famously said there is no hidden God, is now facing the rise of sects commanding millions of members and rather more fervour than the Communist Party. In the twenty-first century we need not be surprised that there are surprises.

The Surprises of Continuity

Yet if these and other events are surprises by dint of what has changed, there are other forms of surprise, in the form of things that have not changed, but have rather continued, contrary to expectations. Not only the 'death' of religion, but also the death of the state, the family and the novel have failed to materialise. In European affairs the sometimes underperforming and contested EU, a visionary project some 50 years ago, has continued to grow. Notwithstanding the initial weakness of the euro, everyone in Europe wants, it seems, to be part of its customs union. Even the UN, for all its weakness, continues: few seriously propose leaving it. More significantly perhaps and of great import for the world as a whole is the stability of power relations between major states. Two decades ago we heard much about the decline of US hegemony and the rise of other, rival, states – Europe, Russia, Japan. Now Russia is in disarray and will probably remain so for decades, Japan has been in an enduring economic crisis since 1990, and Europe is hoping for, at best, some seat at the commercial, financial and strategic military table with the USA as the latter's economy charges ahead. A decade or so ago Paul Kennedy wrote his learned and astute *The Rise and Fall of the Great*

Powers, showing how through over-extension a cycle of rising and falling power had beset past hegemonic or imperial powers – Rome, Holland, Britain – and how this might well affect the USA itself.[5] A decade later, we hear little about US overstretch, more about 'hyper-globalism', the 'indispensable superpower' and unilateralism, matters which will be addressed in Chapter 7.

Human affairs do and will contain surprises, for good and for bad: but these may be as much ones about what does not change as about ones that do. Perhaps a century from now the British will still be suspicious of Brussels, the Irish question – that is, conflicts *between* Irish communities – will not be resolved, fundamentalists of all stripes will claim their culture is under attack from alien conspiracy, and Americans will think the rest of the world is getting a free ride. Perhaps not. We should, however, not assume that all will change, anymore than that our wishes will become reality. To confuse your wishes with reality is, as Macchiavelli rightly said, the greatest mistake in politics, and it is as true in the international sphere as in the domestic. Chapter 10 will address the question of how we can think, imagine, argue for alternative worlds to that which we now have. Such an endeavour is, I shall argue, necessary and desirable. But such alternative thinking, utopian in the best sense, has to be based on a realism. A realism of outlook is, of course, equally directed against the assumption that all can remain the same as it is against impossible and dangerous alternative visions. The first place to start is with a realistic, critical but sober, view of the limits on millennial novelty, of the impact of the past on the world at 2000.

2

The Shadow of the Twentieth Century

The dawn of a new year, let alone a new millennium, is convention-ally accompanied by a sense of drawing a line under the past: the hope is that the tensions and failures that marked the previous time will not recur. In the case of 2000 this is, if anything, all the stronger because of the most marked change associated with the end of the twentieth century, the termination of major inter-state conflict with the end of the cold war. If to this is added a sense of the end of an era of ideological contestation, and an infectious, if not entirely convincing, optimism associated with technological change, then the reasons for moving on, for denying the relevance of the past, may be all the greater.

In some measure this sense of rupture is valid. Much more than the millennium itself, the end of the cold war, in its manifold dimensions, did mark a major strategic and ideological break point in world history. In Eric Hobsbawm's telling formulation, 1991 was very much the conclusion of a 'Short Twentieth Century' which began in 1914.[1] The growth of economic co-operation between major states, and a certain spread of democracy, have compounded this sense of novelty. Yet for states and nations, as for individuals, a denial of the past may only serve to give it even more influence over the present. On the one hand, those who deny the import of history are all the more effectively under its influence. On the other, those who do invoke history always do so, to a greater or lesser extent, selectively and often in self-serving ways: wallowing in national or religious tradition is no way to resolve the past. The twentieth century casts a shadow over the twenty-first as effectively in ways that may not be recognized as in ways that are.

For three important reasons in particular the history of the twentieth century cannot be easily set aside. In the first place, the shape of the twenty-first century world – the map of states, the division of the world along economic lines, the international institutions that comprise global governance, the very disputes that drive so much of the world – was largely shaped by the history of the twentieth. One obvious example is the reluctance of two major economic powers, Germany and Japan, each with large populations, to play commensurate strategic roles – a direct consequence of their reaction against the aggression they perpetrated in the middle of the twentieth. Second, the twentieth century shapes the terms of sentiment, in the ways in which peoples across the world perceive the international system, and the ways in which they regard each other. The rise of community and ethnic consciousness, as of religious sentiment, reflects a mobilization of the twentieth-century past to suit the purposes of the present. On their part, post-imperial nostalgia affects many European states. Third and most substantively, the lived experience of globalization draws on conceptions of power, and inequality, derived from earlier periods – the cold war and, before that, colonialism. Indeed, the whole discourse of conflict within globalization reflects the continued impact of these times, since that very discourse is in large measure phrased in a vocabulary and conceptual system derived from earlier conflicts.

Recognition of the past is not, however, merely a matter of realizing how history shapes the present: it is also, or can also be, part of consciously shaping that present by retaining a memory of that which is positive in the past. Here the legacy of the twentieth century may be as much one that allows for progress and the realization of a potential that was, at enormous costs, sustained in the conflicts of that period. A reflection on the influence of the past may, therefore, serve the present in diverse ways – to lessen the impact of past conflicts and resentments on the present, to recognize the ways in which an apparently new world, that of globalization, is shaped by the past, and to bring into the twenty-first century that democratic potential which was fought for, and sustained, in the twentieth. Not the least important part of such a recognition is the discussion of how Europe, the focus of twentieth-century conflict but also source of many ideals of freedom, can contribute to this reassessment.

The Twentieth Century: a Short History

If the economic history of the twentieth century was one of successive cycles of capitalist expansion and loss of momentum, and its scientific history one of great advance and abuse, its politics were marked by three comprehensive processes – war, revolution and democratization. The first half of the century was dominated by two world wars: these conflicts engulfed almost all of Europe, and much of the Middle and Far East, and brought the hitherto isolated USA into the affairs of both Europe and Asia. The second half of the century was constituted, until 1991, by another, more complex and multidimensional global rivalry, the cold war. Militarily, this was a strategic competition between two blocs: it threatened to destroy humanity in a nuclear nightmare. It was at the same time accompanied by a succession of wars in the Third World that left an estimated 20 million dead: while these wars raged over the Middle East, southern Africa and Latin America, the most intense and lethal of all were in East Asia – China in the late 1940s, Korea from 1950 to 1953, and Vietnam from 1946 to 1975. Of the 20 million estimated to have died in conflict after 1945, 10.4 million died in East Asia, compared to 4 million in sub-Saharan Africa and 2.9 million in Central and South Asia.

The cold war was, above all, an ideological conflict – a clash between two conceptions, and two, heterogeneously organized, social systems – as to how the world should be organized. It had a social, as much as a military or political history. Millions fought, and died, for these rival conceptions. Too easily forgotten in retrospect, or in the pages of structural explanations, is the fact that human agency was central – in the form of ideologies, leaders and organized collective engagement. If, in the closing decade, there were those who doubted whether the cold war was 'about' anything, the scale of the change, and subjugation, visited after the cold war's end on the defeated Soviet bloc should have settled this once and for all. The countries of the former Soviet bloc, and of the former USSR itself, were fundamentally altered by the collapse of communism. This was a change that, to all but those blinded by a facile teleology, amounted to a revolution. In the near 40 years of cold war, each side aspired to victory. In the end, there was a result: one side won.

The most important dates, the punctuation marks of this century, are related to its three constitutive processes: for the world wars, 1914 and 1939, for the revolutions, 1917 and 1949, for democratization, 1945 and 1991. There was, however, no firebreak between these three processes. The two world wars of the first half of the century were caused, above all, by the explosion of social conflict within developing authoritarian states onto the international arena, just as the cold war was sustained by the contradictory, rival diversity of the capitalist and communist systems. At the termination of each of the three world conflicts – 1918, 1945, 1991 – there occurred not just a realignment of the great powers, but also revolutionary political change – after World War I in Russia, after World War II in China, and in other parts of the Third World, and after the cold war in the social, and political, transformation of the former Soviet bloc.

In the view of some observers, there is no pattern in these events. Here anti-foundationalist scepticism and traditional historiography meet – history is, for them, just one event after the other. It may, however, be suggested that there is a certain shape in the century, not one determined from the beginning, any more than is the case in analysing economic history, but one which in retrospect emerges as having occurred. This pattern is above all one of the explosion and then partial resolution of the conflicts associated with modernity, with the growth of industrial society and the tensions within and between society that this unleashed. In the first half of the century the general crisis of modern society exploded into war and revolution; in the second the tensions that matured in the first, and which left their legacy in the cold war, were gradually brought under some political control – democratic within states, diplomatic and multilateral between them.[2]

1945: the Turning Point

In the context of this twentieth-century perspective, the central moment, the turning point, is that of 1945. The importance of this watershed is all the more evident over half a century later, at the end of the twentieth century. Beyond all the significance which states and self-justifying elites wish to impose on 1945, there is one central message suggested by recognition of this turning point: it serves both as a warning and a suggestion of hope. The warning consists in an awareness of the dangers which authoritarian capitalism poses for the world, and which it could still pose in the future. The rise of a conservative and xenophobic right in Austria and Switzerland in the late

1990s, feeding on a revived indulgence of the Nazi past on the one hand and a hostility to immigration on the other, suggests the possibility of an ominous new authoritarian force in European politics. The USA has never been short of such tendencies in regard to social and military issues. In Japan they are muted, but recurrent. The victory of 1945 was, therefore, decisive, but provisional: the potential for authoritarian and racist politics under capitalism remains, from below as from above. As the German philosopher Max Horkheimer put it in 1939, those who do not wish to talk about capitalism, should not talk about fascism – and many do not.[3] That, in the triumphalist atmosphere of the 1990s, was too easily forgotten: memory of the fascist period has been confined to selective indignation, over genocide, rather than applied to the broader programme of social repression and racism within which anti-Semitism was central but which had a much wider ideological and geographical aspiration. The appeal to blood and tradition, the deprecation of other peoples and the constant reformulation of authority are endemic to modern society.

Recognition of 1945 is also an occasion to look forward – to remember, revise, develop a concept of human emancipation. There is an economic history of the twentieth century, as there is a military and a scientific one. But the twentieth century was, as much as anything, the age of politics, the clash of authoritarian and imperial regimes in the first half, the fitful spread of emancipation in the second, the constant conflict between rulers and ruled in which, gradually, and at enormous costs, the ruled gained ground at the expense of their rulers. Too often forgotten is that these advances were the result of collective resistance and protest, not the unfolding of some immanent liberalizing logic, or the gift of benevolent rulers. It was these movements too which redefined, and continue to redefine, what democracy is capable of: from the demand for male suffrage to that for equal male and female voting rights, from a restricted view of the role of states to one in which the state is expected to provide a large measure of welfare, from a conception of rights concentrated on the vote to one in which a range of social and economic entitlements are given legal, if not as yet due, recognition.

For the non-European world, the end of World War II marked the beginnings of the period in which European colonialism was finally brought to an end. This system of domination, had, in its various shapes, formal and informal, encompassed the world since the sixteenth century and, in terms of peoples and territories ruled, reached its height in 1938: at that time around 40% of the world's population was under direct colonial rule. Latin America had shaken off colonialism after the Napoleonic Wars, the empires of Europe – Romanov, Ottoman, Hapsburg, and (in the case of Ireland) British – had been dissolved after World War I. World War II shattered this system elsewhere, at once by weakening the power and resolve of the European colonial powers, even when they emerged as victors, as by mobilizing the peoples of these countries in new forms of revolt and nationalist aspiration. In the Middle East, the rise of nationalist movements in Iran and the Arab world was a response to the upheavals provoked by World War II. In the subcontinent, British rule ended in 1947. Nowhere was this impact of world events more evident than in East Asia. World War II transformed China and, with the defeat of Japan, created the context for the revolution that was to triumph in 1949. In Vietnam, the removal of French colonialism and the sudden paralysis of Japan, in August 1945, allowed the Vietnamese communists to take control of the whole country: they were to spend the next 30 years seeking to retain and regain that independence from French and American interventions. In the second most populous country in the East Asia, Indonesia, Dutch rule was brought rapidly to a close in the nationalist uprising of 1945–49. In Africa, the late 1940s and 50s were to see the rise of nationalist movements, from Algiers to Cape Town, that were to challenge the pattern of European domination and, in the case of Portugal in 1974, to provoke political revolution in the metropolitan centre itself.

As far as Europe was concerned, the liberation in 1945 from fascism of all the continent bar Spain and Portugal benefited the continent as a whole, not least the peoples of the former fascist states themselves. It marked the end of a conflict, the most bloody in human history, that had been justified by the anti-fascist alliance in the name of freedom. Yet, as the ensuing 50 years showed, that liberation concealed within it the contradictions of the modern concept of freedom, and above all the contest between two warped competitors for emancipation. World War II was a war fought by two rival inheritors of the Enlightenment, imperialist capitalism and anti-imperialist communism, against a third force, authoritarian and racist capitalism. This authoritarian capitalism sought to deny that Enlightenment, even as it profited from the technologies and ideas of modernity. It rose to power on the very social and political conflicts that modernity itself had generated, above all in World War I and in the inter-war period.

The history of the world since 1945 was, until 1991, dominated by the cold war, the competition between these two modernistic projects, communism and capitalism. The original hopes of 1945, of a single emancipatory project continuing the project of the wartime alliance, and epitomized in the aspirations of anti-fascist coalitions, the UN from above, popular front from below, were soon confounded. Yet, for all the freezing of the cold war, emancipation continued. The defeat of fascism in Germany, Italy and Japan led to the establishment of prosperous and, within strikingly divergent limits, democratic regimes: whatever else, they ceased to be military threats to their neighbours. The impact of World War II on the European colonial states, combined with pressure from both the USSR and the USA, led within the space of two decades to the ending of the European colonial empires. The fear of revolt from below, and above all communism, prompted social reform throughout the west. In the 1960s, within western Europe a series of emancipatory movements, many influenced, paradoxically, by the emergence of radical social and cultural trends within the USA, came increasingly to contest established systems of hierarchy and power, not least those of gender. The USA itself underwent a radical democratization in the era of the civil rights movement.

In the 1970s, the authoritarian regimes of the right, entrenched in Spain and Portugal and more recently reconsolidated in Greece, crumbled in the face of democratic and social pressures within, and the example of a democratic *and* prosperous world without. Finally, and most dramatically, at the end of the l980s the contest between these two distorted forms of emancipation ended in the crumbling of the authoritarian regimes of the left: unable to prevail over its liberal democratic rival, and, even more importantly, unable to evolve into a democratic form capable of realizing an alternative political model, the systems of bureaucratic communism collapsed, with merciful speed and passivity. Communism offered a future that was *beyond* the existing order, a *post-capitalist* stage in what was seen as a set of historical stages, but in aspiration, and the underlying view of history, it was mistaken. It failed to do better than capitalism, in economic or political terms. It mistook its own concerted and world-wide challenge for a definitive higher phase of history. Above all, it forgot the secret of modernity that Marx himself had so well identified in 1848, that of constant change: there was no single-track historical achievement to be 'constructed'. The very goals that communism set itself in its early challenge to capitalism, after 1917, ceased to be the decisive ones decades later. Modernity dug the grave of a static communism, not that of an ever-changing capitalism.

Events after 1991 were, in all their diversity, determined by the disintegration of that conflict between communism and capitalism, the cold war. Three distinct processes were condensed into that one disintegration: the collapse of the USSR, and of other multinational states, and the emergence of over 20 new independent countries; the ending of the strategic, military rivalry of the great powers, and the receding of the danger of nuclear war; the end of the great ideological divide, between proponents of the existing system and its reform, and advocates of a revolutionary alternative, which had prevailed for 200 years. As we shall see in Chapter 3, this new period has occasioned a mass of alternative analyses: yet the broad outlines of the years since the end of cold war are clear enough: a consolidation of the power of the OECD states economically, through increased US hegemony on the one hand, and the advance of European integration on the other; the incorporation, under chaotic conditions, of the former Soviet and east European states into the capitalist world economy; the gradual, unresolved, economic integration of China; spasmodic, but thwarted, attempts by authoritarian regimes to exploit the new international uncertainties; the dispersal of resistance, collective and individual, by Third World countries to domination by the west. Here, too, the surprises may be as much in the predictable as in the unexpected.

'European' Values and Beyond

The resolution in 1991 of the rivalry between two social systems was accompanied, as already discussed in Chapter 1, by the early stages of a potentially tectonic change in the map of world power. The twentieth century began with a dramatic defeat for Europe, in the Russo-Japanese War of 1904–05; the last years of the twentieth century were marked by the final end, fitful but inexorable, of five centuries of European domination of the world, evident above all in the shift of economic power from the Atlantic to the Far East. The British withdrawal from Hong Kong in June 1997 marked, as clearly as any one point could, the final end of this half millennium of European colonial expansion. Yet this very shift requires an assessment of Europe's place in that history. The two world wars, and the cold war, were, for all their global impact, generated in Europe. It is the outcome of these histories for Europe that has above all determined the significance of the twentieth century, one shaped by the contradictory character of Europe's place in modern history.

The negative dimensions of this European record should never be forgotten. At the start of the twenty-first century there is no place for piety about the defence of 'European' values: recent work on the history of slavery and colonialism has re-emphasized the role of murder, disease and plunder in the earlier European subjugation of the world.[4] At the same time, the greatest crimes of the twentieth century, and the most inhuman ideas of our history, notably racism, were generated in Europe. The European authoritarianisms of right and left destroyed millions of people in the name of their historical vision. For their part, the liberal democracies, more benign at home, visited destruction on the Third World, through colonialism and post-colonial wars, that added many more millions to the avoidable toll of the twentieth century.

In contemporary discussion, an invocation of 'European identity' has also too often a racist subtext, be this in regard to Islamic peoples, or as was exemplified in the post-1992 wars of the Balkans: here such an invocation of the European past, and identity, by Serbs and Croats, was irretrievably linked to sectarian and genocidal projects, the former against Muslims, the latter against Serbs. More generally Europe is constructed in terms of negatives: factitious use of a supposed need for an 'other', derived sometimes from a misreading of anthropology, sometimes from unduly revered conservative writers such as Carl Schmitt, has served these purposes. Sometimes this 'other' is defined as the Islamic world, or, in misapplied philosophical mode, as 'Islam', sometimes it is associated with the Third World as a whole. In reality, Europe has had many 'others': the most long-standing has been Persia, the 'other' that defined classical Greece, while the most formative extra-European power of all has been the USA, a more influential and challenging alterity than any other. Most significantly of all, the two major drives of European history over the past half millennium, economic and strategic expansion outwards, and internecine war within, have both been independent of any 'other'. The former, economic growth and the Industrial Revolution, was largely endogenous, driven from within; the latter had remarkably little relation to the non-European world, be it in terms of competition for raw materials or strategic rivalry. The 'other' is convenient, as apologia and source of plunder, not determinant.

This history, European and global, reinforces an awareness of the contradictory character of modernity itself – evident in the rivalries of the authoritarian left and right that dominated the second half of the century, and in the many conflicts that constitute societies, and relations between societies, today. As will be explored in later chapters, such an awareness should warn against many of the simplistic theories that are being generated to explain the post-cold-war world. The threat of authoritarian regression, as of renewed inter-state military rivalry, hangs over the onset of the twenty-first century as it did, casting a shadow on the horizon of modish optimism, *la belle époque,* a century ago. The 'End of History', expounded by Francis Fukuyama, ignores the uneven, and itself contradictory, spread of economic integration and political change.[5] While Fukuyama is right to claim that history is, for the moment, static, in the sense that no ideology of global aspiration exists to challenge that of liberal capitalism, no one can be sure that this situation will endure in part because of another factor that Fukuyama rightly stresses, the human need for respect, or *thymos.* The great majority of humanity does not live under democratic, or advanced industrial, conditions. Indeed, as the underside of the prosperity and growth of recent years, the gap between the developed 10% of the world's population and the rest has grown throughout this century, and continues to do so. The complacently celebrated 'triumph of the west' therefore ignores the historic destructiveness of the west, the growing inequality within contemporary globalization and the rise of economic centres that reject the mid-Atlantic hegemonies of the past half millennium.

Yet much of modernity and part of what is of universal, not restrictedly regional, value in terms of political liberties arose in Europe. This is, in two important respects, not the same as seeing them as products of the 'west'. First of all, the core values of a democratic world – rights, independence, equality, democracy itself – share both a European and a non-European provenance. As with the roots of much modern science and mathematics, they draw on older, non-European elements. The concept of '0' or zero, central to the digital revolution of today, was taken by European mathematics from India in the eleventh century. Second, the values of democracy were given their modern formulation not by a hegemonic or imperial elite, but in the upheavals that themselves convulsed Europe in the eighteenth and nineteenth centuries. The crystallization of these ideas was a product not of some undifferentiated 'west' but of the social and political conflicts and movements for emancipation within the west. As we shall see in the discussion of 'anti-imperialism' in Chapter 3 and Chapter 10, to reject this legacy as unacceptably 'Eurocentric', or 'ethnocentric', a product of some undifferentiated hegemonic narrative, is to lose an important element in the emancipatory legacy of humanity as a whole.[6]

There is a further risk in such a rejection: it may concede, in the name of relativist uncertainty, to forms of oppression, justified in nationalist terms. Not all that is oppressive is derived from hegemony: any assessment of oppression and denial of rights has to combine denunciation of that which is exogenous, imperial or hegemonic, and that which is endogenous, nativist and instrumentally 'authentic'. Those with power – social, political, gendered, religious, possibly all together – can, and do, use this rhetoric of rejection of 'western' values to legitimate their own forms of domination. Nor, as will be explored in Chapter 7, should we accept at face value claims that one 'western' system of values is distinct from, or incompatible with, that which is counterposed to it. In both historical form, through cultural and scientific interaction, and in the context of the modern world, what appear as distinct cultures or discourses may have much more in common. The strength of multitudinous ethnic and religious movements often conceals their appropriation of modernistic ideas and preconditions: no national or cultural movement rejects the principle of national self-determination, or the right of nations to participate in the World Cup. Relativism is very much a selective process. This should, if anything, reinforce the defence of universal values such as tolerance and reason, appropriated from below and which to a considerable degree were formulated in Europe, and the conflicts it generated.

The twentieth century is not, therefore, an epoch that can or should be forgotten: in terms of structuring the world of states, economies and peoples it retains a formative influence; it has bequeathed, often in ways that are not recognized, the ideas and passions of the contemporary world; above all else, it has provided, through the social upheavals and wars that marked it, a political agenda that is far from complete and which may form the basis for addressing the problems of the future.

3
Arguments about World Politics

The end of the cold war and the prevalence of globalization have occasioned not only millennial optimism but many a grand theory, a carnival of competing generalizations among writers on international affairs as to how to characterize the contemporary world. Globalization is conventionally portrayed as producing uniformity, but in the domain of ideas at least it has produced diversity of meta-historical claims. Some writers such as Robert Kaplan have seen the world after 1989 as a reversal, a return to the past, or a resurgence of 'the repressed', especially in ethnic and religious terms.[1] Others such as Zaki Laidi have seen 1989 as ushering in 'a world crisis of meaning', or what he terms a 'gigantic semantic cemetery, where words, scarcely having been used and popularized, lose their meaning and then fall into obscurity'.[2] Both approaches may make their mark by intuition, but may lose by excess of generalization. Elsewhere there is a more articulated, but as ever debatable, set of alternative visions, a variety of competing approaches to the contemporary world, and to global governance. For the sake of convenience we may analyse them in terms of four schools, somewhat simplified or ideal types perhaps, but not that far from the range of contemporary debate about the international system.

Hegemonic Optimism

The first, and within the OECD most prevalent, view is hegemonic optimism. This is the view that with the collapse of communism, and the spread of globalization, the world is on the verge of a new, triumphal age, one in which political liberalism, market economics

and the advances of science, particularly the life sciences and information technology, will usher in a new epoch. This approach has
been ably articulated by Francis Fukuyama and Thomas Friedman.[3]
In variant form the notions of the 'End of History', the 'New World
Order', the 'Triumph of the Market' all represent this outlook as does,
in more nationalistic vein, renewed talk of the 'American Century', a
concept originally coined by Henry Luce in 1941. According to this
approach, those major states which are opposed to the western variant
of hegemony, Russia and China, are holding out for a better deal – on
strategic weapons, or WTO membership and will, sooner or later, fall
into line. Of course there remain problems – pockets of poverty and
crime within the developed countries, poverty in some areas of the
Third World that have not yet made the transition, states variously
classed as 'rogue' or 'pariah' who refuse to comply. Overall,
however, a juggernaut is sweeping the world and it is basically a
good thing. All that remains is, in the Hegelian phrase, 'the realignment of the provinces'.

This, it should be noted, is a far cry from what had, until the end
of the cold war, been the dominant approach to the international
system among those controlling states, namely the balance of power:
this meant not that an actual balance existed, but rather that international politics operated by a process of balancing, whereby the
preponderance of any one state was offset by the countervailing
power, or coalition, of others. The balance of power was, in this
sense, a self-correcting mechanism which operated against those,
such as Napoleon and Hitler, who aspired to dominate Europe, and,
in the cold war, the world. It entailed, however, a world dominated
by strategic rivalry. Today the balance of power would only continue
to operate if an alternative to the USA as a major power emerged.
This appears to be improbable for a long time to come: hence the
attractions of hegemonic optimism.[4]

Hegemonic optimism is, not to over-simplify, the view of the
major leaders of the OECD states, it is the world view proclaimed in
the house journals of global hegemony – *The Economist*, the *International Herald Tribune*, the *Financial Times* and their counterparts
in each country. This is the view you get from watching CNN. These
journals and media are not, as their critics too easily allege, peddling
lies, or engaged in some vast conspiracy to stop 'us', the virtuous
people, from getting at 'the truth'. They are in the main well
informed, and intelligent, and would need to be: if you are running

a company or a state, or a region, let alone aspiring to co-ordinate the running of the world, you need to be flexible, and well informed, and to be so on time. Media commentators need to be on the mark as far as finance, technology, mergers, as well as art markets, *feng shui*, film, shifts in gender relations, frequent traveller tips and the rest are concerned.

The problems are, however, several. First of all, the bases for international co-operation to address the challenges of the contemporary world are in large measure absent. The 'New World Order' proclaimed by US President George Bush in 1991 lasted a few months: it rested on American–Soviet collaboration through the UN that was swept aside, first by the collapse of the USSR and then by disputes within the UN between the western states, particularly the USA and Britain on the one hand and Russia and China on the other. The twentieth century ended with discord among the great powers over Kosovo, growing disquiet in eastern *and* western Europe about US missile intentions, and diffuse, if unduly muted, disgust at Russian atrocities in Chechnya. When we come to other major international fora, agreement is also elusive: because of disputes between states the world is further than ever from effective regulation of such issues as the environment or narcotics. The same applies to the WTO: the main story at Seattle in late November 1999 was not what happened on the streets. The 35,000 protesters, and the minority committed to ruckus and trashing Condé Nast and Starbucks, were not the main reason why the WTO conference failed: it failed because of disagreement between states – between the USA and the Europeans on the one hand, and between the OECD states and a coalition of Third World countries including Brazil, Egypt and India on the other.

When it comes to security issues, the situation is even less reassuring: the regime of non-proliferation and test ban renunciation built up over decades collapsed at the end of the twentieth century in the twin thunderclaps of the South Asian explosions of 1998 and the US Senate's rejection of the CTBT in 1999. Another attempt to control nuclear missiles, the Non-Proliferation Treaty, was first signed in 1968 and has, since 1995, been extended indefinitely, with a review every five years. The world's nations agreed at the NPT review conference in New York in April 2000 to set a long-term goal of nuclear disarmament: we may doubt if that meets even the most charitable version of plausibility. Chapter 4 will return to this theme.

A second problem with hegemonic optimism is the structurally unequal, oligarchic character of the contemporary international economy, and of globalization in particular. As we shall see in Chapter 5, the world is more and more unequal: 68% of world investment and trade is within the top 20% of the world's economy: the income gap between the top 20% of the world and the bottom 20% now stands at 86:1. International public discussion represents the world view of a small elite, less than 10% of the world's population. In the news, analysis and above all the opinion columns of global media, there is far too little, almost no, reflection of the experience and feelings of the rest of the world's population. Some columnists do express outrage and concern but the feelings of the majority of the peoples of the world are not adequately reflected: their own leaders posture but do not in the main respond. We read of the crisis of currencies, much less of what this means to those affected in the ensuing months and years. Whether it be in regard to the social effects of economic restructuring, or of the information revolution, or of western military actions justified on humanitarian grounds, the range of debate reflected by this OECD elite is narrow indeed.

Those of a realist orientation may be tempted to ask 'so what?': the developed world can build a wall around itself and foray outside for occasional needs such as oil and tourism. But, even leaving all ethical issues aside, this was never, and is decreasingly, a possibility: what Robert Cooper has termed the pre-modern world, and much of the modern, can take its toll on the post-modern through pressures of migration, through military, including chemical and biological – and, perhaps in the future environmental and epidemiological – challenges.[5] Saddam Hussein and the East Asian financial crisis were examples of a unified and interdependent world. Fortress OECD is *not* an option.

Third, as will be explored in Chapter 6, the two pillars of the hegemonic optimistic view – democracy and the market – do not hold together in the way their protagonists suggest. Democracy is not sweeping the world: rather we see a contested consolidation of democracy for at most a quarter of the world's population, and a range of semi-authoritarian states for the rest. The very survival of democracy in those states in which it is established is contingent on long-term public support and commitment and is threatened in new ways by technological change. Elsewhere, the term 'emerging democracies' is another teleological myth. To talk of 'transition' is to presume that something is going to happen, when it may not. As for the market, it is driving economies in western Europe, but not in many other places. As a result of the collapse of communism, GDP fell by, on average, over a half in the former Soviet countries: in the whole of eastern Europe only in Poland did GDP in 1999 reach the levels of 1989. The fluctuations of share and currency markets, driven by belief in the transformations brought on by the Internet, run the risk of promoting other sudden speculative crises.

Above all, the hegemonic optimists run the risk of forgetting one of the greatest lessons of the twentieth century: this is not only that revolt from below alters history, but that it is also the failure of those ruling which also opens the door to instability. Change comes from below *and* above. Indeed, all the great transitional moments of the last century were the result, first and foremost, of the failures of those with power: 1914 destroyed the previous era of peace and led to the Russian Revolution of 1917 and the fall of most of the ruling houses in Europe; the Nazis came to power in 1933 because of the great depression and the disunity of the German political elite; the collapse of communism in 1989 resulted from a loss of confidence, and direction from the top, within the USSR. The wars of the former Yugoslavia were produced by conflict between different sections of the communist elite. The same thing may happen again: the onward march of globalization, and the system of global governance as we know it, are threatened as much by the incompetence and frivolous disputation of those in power as by the challenge of those without. Trends towards unilateralism in international affairs, and disunity within global institutions, suggest the same prospect of instability from above may recur. To take an obvious example: the outside world has protested, and is protesting, about the rising nationalistic determination by the USA to destroy the 1972 Anti-ballistic Missile (ABM) regime. The deployment by a future US administration of some system of anti-ballistic missiles will have long-term destabilizing effects: its goal is not Iran or Korea, but China and Russia. Deployment could well happen, and the consequences may be enormous. Hegemonic optimism may, in the 2000s as in the 1900s, be an illusion of those whose actions are doing the most to undermine it.

Liberal Reform

A second approach to the contemporary international situation, and to global governance in particular, is that of liberal reform, relying above all on international institutions such as the UN and growing co-operation between developed states.[6] The fiftieth anniversary of the UN, in 1995, was a high point for such a perspective: hundreds of reports were produced on strengthening the international governance system. The millennium occasioned a further round of prospective advocacy, including a special UN General Assembly session in September 2000. Prime among the sets of proposals occasioned by the fiftieth anniversary was the Commission on Global Governance's report *Our Global Neighbourhood*. It and other reports made such proposals as reforming the Security Council, establishing a comparable Economic Council, incorporating NGOs more actively into the system, and fostering a global ethic with regard to conflict, rights, the environment, migration. At its simplest, this liberal reformism involves the belief that, for all their shortcomings, the institutions that we now have, from the UN through to the EU and regional organizations, can and should be developed and strengthened. We need, it is argued, to take further the strengthening of international institutions and supplement them with a greater commitment and responsibility. Building on the vision of those who founded the UN and the EU amidst the global rubble of World War II, the world should, in a word, try harder.

There are, as we shall see in greater detail in Chapter 9, a range of problems with this approach too. First of all, it ignores the history of the past 50 years: international institutions have worked only to the extent, and on the issues, where the dominant states within them wish them to work. They have not been allowed to adjudicate effectively in relation to major states, nor have they been active against the wishes of those states. This is the lesson which the UN learned and which, despite much integrationist rhetoric, the EU is learning again: the big players count, and, where they want to, obstruct. In 1966 French President de Gaulle stated, 'Europe is an affair of the French and Germans combined'[7] – a third of a century later there is no reason to revise this judgement. The strand of liberal reformism to which current thinking inclines has itself not fared well: few remember the Brandt Commission of 1980 with its detailed proposals for a programme of global Keynesianism and the implementation of a

'New International Economic Order' (NIEO). The NIEO got almost nowhere, partly because of the refusal of Third World states to co-operate with each other on any commodity other than oil, more importantly because of the refusal of the OECD states to enter into meaningful negotiation: for the record, the NIEO hit a brick wall at the Cancun Conference of developed and developing states of October 1981. The only component of it that was in some measure implemented were the guarantees, pretty feeble ones at that, contained in the Lomé Convention, negotiated between the EU and its 60 or so former colonial territories: that was dismantled in the neo-liberal years that followed, although renewed in depleted form in June 2000. The EU market share of those countries fell from 6.7% in 1976 to 3% in 1998. The goals of other reports, including the Brundt-land Report on the environment, were, in large measure, also ignored.

The priorities of powerful states have been strongly evident too in another much discussed domain, that of peacekeeping and humani-tarian intervention. This was, par excellence, the role which liberal internationalism saw the UN and its members performing and which the end of the cold war at first appeared to make possible. Liberal opinion has, since the end of the cold war, been divided on this. Each case of intervention, from Kuwait to Kosovo, has occasioned dispute. The predominant view within the liberal community has been *in favour* of actions to preserve peace and human rights. The problem has been the very partial record of response – non-existent in some cases (Rwanda, Afghanistan), belated in others (East Timor, Bosnia), abandoned under pressure (Somalia), without political reso-lution (Kuwait, Haiti). The great optimism of the early 1990s, embodied in Boutros-Ghali's *Agenda for Peace* (1992), foundered in the agonies of Mogadishu, Sarajevo and Srebrenica, and the indeci-siveness and wishful thinking of the Security Council itself.

A second dimension of the liberal reformist position is the emphasis on NGOs and, more broadly, on the construction of a global civil society made up of reform-oriented groups. NGOs are an important feature of the contemporary world and some have made a significant contribution to the formulation and diffusion of a liberal agenda: the role of Amnesty International, Oxfam and Greenpeace is indisputable. Some campaigns – not least that against anti-personnel weapons – have had their impact. The issue of the environment was placed on the global agenda by the work of writers and lobbies in the 1980s and 90s. But the significance of, and opportunities for, NGOs should not be overstated. The romance of NGOs is, and should be, coming to an end. In the first place, NGOs are not, and cannot be, a substitute for states: most NGOs seek not to replace states but to get them to work more effectively for their goals, on human rights or whatever; many receive significant proportions of their income from states and are to a considerable degree contractors for them – and hence subject to their political prohibitions. Some, of course, have wished themselves to become states – guerrilla nationalist forces such as the PLO, FRETILIN, the ANC. In other cases states devolve onto civil society functions that they no longer wish to fulfil.

NGOs posit themselves as a more democratic and/or effective form of governance, but they may evade criteria of governance themselves: it is often hard to say how representative, or efficient, or democratic they are. The internal governance of NGOs ranges across a wide spectrum – and is on occasion beset by inefficiency defended as self-righteousness. NGOs talk in the name of a self-proclaimed constituency, but sometimes this is, and sometimes it is not, democratically constituted. Nor should we be bemused, by a diffuse scepticism about states, into thinking that all that is 'non-governmental' is benign or even wishes to be: at the Beijing Women's Conference in 1995 Amnesty drew up a classification of NGOs ranging from genuine INGOs (international NGOs), through BINGOs (business-supported NGOs), RINGOs (religious and often conservative NGOs), to GINGOs (government-controlled NGOs), of which there are many.[8] Middle Eastern commentators have added TINGOs (tribal NGOs). The world of the non-governmental encompasses the liberal and the benevolent, but also includes Opus Dei, a conservative Catholic body that has set as its goal the covert domination of the EU, the drugs cartels, the Mafia, and sundry illiberal groups that have emerged from the former communist countries.

There remains a strand of optimism, but also naivety, about the liberal agenda in regard to international organizations. Some examples may suffice: a permanent UN peacekeeping force, a second general assembly encompassing NGOs and/or popular representatives, open diplomacy, an end to controls on human mobility. These are fine objectives but they ignore the world in which we live. The Permanent Five members of the Security Council may support a stronger peacekeeping staff in New York but are not on present form going to set up, or finance, a permanent peacekeeping force: indeed they have made sure that, under current practices, contingents with the UN in, say, Bosnia or Kosovo remain almost wholly under national command. The goal of an independent UN force, above all one with an independent chain of command, is a mirage. A second general assembly would be even more ineffective, more of a talking shop, than the existing one and would have even less impact. An assembly of NGOs would invite the question of how representative these bodies are. An elected assembly, on a one person one vote basis, would give a majority to China and India that others would reject.

Open negotiation and discussion is one of the oldest chimeras of the liberal agenda – it is a recurrent theme in the classic study of liberal critics of power politics, A.J.P. Taylor's *The Troublemakers*:[9] those appointed to negotiate should be democratically chosen and their conclusions ratified in a democratic manner. But open diplomacy may not always be desirable: one suspects that even the most modest successes of international diplomacy over recent years would not have got as far as they did had this open policy been pursued. Certainly none of the arms control agreements of the great powers, or compromises in such inter-ethnic contexts as Ireland, Palestine and South Africa would have reached a conclusion if guarantees of confidentiality had not been given.

As for opening frontiers to a free movement of peoples worldwide, the articulation of a regime for, and the management of, migration is one that most liberal agendas avoid.[10] The easy question – how to treat people, be they political or economic migrants, *once* they have entered a country – is simpler to address. A case for completely open borders is high-minded but irresponsible. The difficult question to confront is how to envisage a negotiated system, a global regime, for migration that meets economic necessity, in both labour exporting and importing countries alike, and moral obligations for those who seek political asylum. The economic arguments, for Europe and Japan, are powerful but face heavy opposition from public opinion. The USA is the one developed country which has adjusted to this, with a mixture of legal, and illegal, immigration; all the others are in various forms of denial and will do too little and too late.

In regard to political asylum, there *is* an international regime: the moral and legal obligations are extensive and would, if taken to their logical conclusion, be momentous. The 1951 UN Convention Relating to the Status of Refugees stipulates in Article 1 that those who face 'a well-founded fear of being persecuted for reasons of race, religion, nationality, membership of a particular social group or political opinion' have the right to asylum. Article 33 states that contracting states shall neither expel nor return applicants. To take the case of applicants for political asylum from the Middle East: if we include ethnic and gender oppression as forms of persecution, as we should, then of the 350 million people in the Middle East it can be argued that only Askhenazi males, and the 25 or so heads of state who exercise supreme and arbitrary power, would be excluded. All the rest of the population of the Middle East could therefore apply for political asylum elsewhere, as could the whole population of China and many another state. The longer-run solution is evident – democratization in the countries of origin. In the meantime, and it promises to be a very long and brutal meantime, this is, perhaps, the most pervasive and visceral issue of all in the contemporary world, for those many millions who, for economic or political reasons, seek to migrate to more fortunate societies.

Beneath liberal reformism there lies an optimistic moral imagination, a hopeful but potentially risky failure to address what is an underlying problem about moral choice in the international arena, the identification of a clear international interest in terms of which moral choices can be made. For all the proclamation of a global interest, there is serious question as to whether, in most areas, such an interest exists. On migration, the environment, drugs, security, distribution of wealth, the organization of higher education, or the distribution of technology differences of interest may, and will, persist. These need management and adjudication more than wishful denial: there is no ideal solution, to aspire to or in the name of which to denounce other measures. As E.H. Carr forcibly argued in *The Twenty Years' Crisis 1919–39*,[11] the liberal view of international relations also assumes that in issues that are in dispute there is some underlying solution that will meet all needs, some harmony of interests, and of moral concerns, that will optimize outcomes for all. This may, but may not, be the case. When it comes to territory, trade, the environment, let alone the tensions between individual and communal or state rights, or to the rights and wrongs of intervention, there may be *no* easy ethical stance. In conflict situations there may often be a conflict between different ethical or legal priorities. This is not to say that international relations are a zero-sum game, but rather that maximizing outcomes may involve difficult, and contested, choices.

A New Anti-imperialism

A more radical or, to use a contemporary term, 'robust' form of critique of the present international system is one that bases itself on the rejection of global governance, and of western control thereof, as 'imperialism'. Such a critique is widespread in the Third World, where it can take forms both analytic and militant. Here the shadows of colonialism and the cold war are much in evidence. The anti-imperialist critique is widespread too within developed countries, in debates on, for example, the crises in Kuwait in 1990, Bosnia in 1995, and Kosovo in 1999, and on the World Bank and the IMF. The provenance of such a critique is multiple: some of it derives from the established, or traditional, left, some from a post-modernist rejection of 'the Enlightenment Project', some from the newer anti-hegemonic social movements that have emerged from the environmental and other social movements. Lenin and radical greens, Mao and the Seattle protesters combine in a broad rejection of a western hegemonic and imperialist project. Thus we hear not only of globalization as a form of imperialism, or American domination, but of the 'imperialism of human rights'. Kuwait and Kosovo were, it is claimed, forms of imperialism, as is the attempt, much indulged in by liberal commentators, to distinguish legitimate and illegitimate war. The 'just war tradition', which has in the past legitimated wars of national liberation and national defence, is now cast as some newly formulated apologia for imperialism.[12]

If we look around the world today these critics are, arguably, the most influential opponents of western hegemony. The diffusion of Noam Chomsky's work is, arguably, an index of this.[13] So too is Edward Said's principled, but misjudged, critique of the 1993 Oslo Agreements between Israel and the PLO. No doubt too the enthusiasm and ease with which such 'anti-imperialist' arguments are adopted testifies to the depth of resentment provoked by western hegemonic power.[14] Over the months before and after the millennium we saw this articulated on the streets of London, Washington, Seattle and elsewhere. Those who, in western newspapers and seminars, discussed in finely discriminating terms the rights and wrongs of, say, the Kuwait, Bosnia and Kosovo operations and who, linked to the UN, aspired to a greater global humanitarian order on the cusp of the third millennium, paid too little attention to this alternative, critical vision. The community of those who study international relations became very enthusiastic over this period about the new international humanitarian regime.

There are, however, major problems with the new anti-imperialism, a widespread and perhaps rather too comfortable global rejectionism. It could, indeed, be suggested that the predominant complacency of the powerful is here matched by an equally complacent anti-imperialism of the critics. Off-the-shelf rejection, anti-western posturing, or waffly environmental fantasizing present as little prospect for an alternative order, intellectual or moral, as endorsement of the power system itself.

In the first place, it has to be asked in the name of what alternative this critique is being made. The prevalent modes of anti-imperialism fail, in broad terms, to address the criterion of practicality. One cannot denounce global capitalism in the name of a possible alternative, a concerted anti-capitalism, if that option is not reasonably plausible. This is all the more so if one alternative, central planning, has had a good run for its money over eight decades of the twentieth century and today holds out in its redoubts – Cuba, North Korea – little hope, or inspiration, to the rest of humanity. Equally, some of the alternatives proposed by the green movement are unrealistic and undesirable: a general invocation of 'nature', or denunciation of technology and industry, are vapid.

There is, moreover, in this approach a naivety about the system of governance itself. The western consensus is treated as too negative, and incapable of positive outcomes, and the opposition treated as too positive. Here the ethical free-fire zone characteristic of much international discussion comes into its own. The World Bank, or the Clinton administration, were, no doubt, responsible for great mistakes and oversights. But they also sought, and in some cases achieved, significant changes in the world. The Blair government in Britain did not meet a full 'ethical' agenda but its record on several issues was substantial, not least the detention of Augusto Pinochet. An ethical over-simplification combines with an analytic one: the formation of western policy is too easily reduced to a single deformative source – the corrupt policy intelligentsia, the military-industrial complex, MNCs in general. A denunciation of hegemonic policy is far too rarely combined with an informed, detailed analysis of how that policy is made. All too often conspiracy theory prevails.

There is also a recurrent naivety about the anti-imperialists. Those opposed to the dominant power structure – be it imperialism, the west, the 'Washington consensus' or whatever else – are not themselves always embodiments of emancipatory values: Saddam Hussein, Slobodan Milosevic, the PKK, sundry ranting clergymen, the Chechen *mujahidin* are entitled to reasonable, just treatment in the world, but not to uncritical support. The insurgents of Chiapas in Mexico attracted much international sympathy when they emerged in 1994 as opponents of capitalist globalization: but their own alternative remains opaque and their substantive relation to the mass of Mexicans obscure. One cannot also ignore that within some NGO culture itself, let alone with the outer reaches of the environmental movement, standards of free speech and accountability, let alone freedom to reject community and tradition, are rather scarce.

We need, however, to get to the central anti-imperialist assumption about power in the international system: this rests upon a widespread, if often unstated, view of the formation of the contemporary world. There is, pervading much of this anti-imperialist literature, a simplistic, arguably one-dimensional and conspiratorial, view of western policy and indeed of the 'west' itself. This is presented as a unitary, coherent, purposive actor, with at its core a hegemonic project: in reality, as explored in the discussion of 'European' values in Chapter 2, there are conflicting, if not contradictory forces at play, now as over the past 200 years, which allow for different interpretations of the 'western' message. A history of domination on one side is matched by one of rights and contestation on the other. There is no one 'west', in historical impact or in ideology. Nor is there one other 'non-western' world with which it interacts. Forces such as nationalism, civil society, movements for gender rights and NGOs increasingly connect the two. Nationalism, movements of the urban and rural poor and women's movements in non-western societies are not western imports, but are rather forces generated within these societies themselves even as they use a language of protest pioneered in the west. They combine international and domestic forms of protest and ideology. Nor is such mobilization solely a matter of opposing domination from outside: these societies themselves are no strangers, in practice and value, to both indigenous domination and opposition.

There are within non-western societies forms of organization, and traditionally validated values introduced, which can combine with, and enhance, emancipatory values from outside; the right to revolt, the conditionality of rulers, the autonomy of political and social spaces, the rights of women, the authority of independent writers, secularism, the validation of multiculturalism – all can be found in the cultures of non-western society, and can combine with such emancipatory trends that have emerged in the west. The very principles that lie at the heart of the concept of rights – the moral worth of the individual, the right to revolt – are found in the great Middle Eastern religions from which the modern, secular vision of rights is derived.

At the heart of the anti-imperialist critique lies, however, something else, a rejection of 'reformism' and engagement with the existing power structures in the name of some supposed 'revolutionary' alternative: it is this which validates the denunciation of negotiation, compromise and accommodation. The distinction between revolution and reform assumes that a programme of change, a set of global aspirations and demands phrased in terms of the non-revolutionary, is by its very nature insufficient, because it does not go beyond tinkering with existing power structures. But this rejection may itself be subject to the critique of history. For it has, in the history of the past century, been revolutions which have turned out to have had limited, set agendas which, once achieved, led to sclerosis. In politics, economics, interpersonal relations, even design it was the USSR in which progress was frozen, and constructed on aspirations that were subsequently overtaken. Communism sought to emulate capitalism in an international, indeed global, competition: but it ignored the most central of all Marxist insights, the ever-changing and expanding character of that capitalism. It was communism, not capitalism, that paid the final price for Marx's insight that 'all that is solid melts into air'. By contrast, the capacity of reform to renew itself is evident throughout the developed world. Equally pertinent, and again challenging the frozen dichotomy of reform and revolution, is the very *inexhaustible* nature of the reform programme itself. The goals of the American and French Revolutions, enshrined in their programme of rights, and linked to a slow, but so far sustained, process of democratization, have not only inspired much of the world in the ensuing two centuries, but also remain far from realized. Indeed, they constitute a marker against which all existing societies and political systems still fail. They would, if realized, lead to a profound, and one could certainly say, revolutionary change in existing orders, a point to which we shall, in Chapter 10, return.

The 'New Middle Ages'

An alternative form of pessimism, of a kind associated historically with the right, but no longer so confined, is that which sees the contemporary world as heading towards a new form of chaos, often termed the 'New Middle Ages': Alain Minc, Robert Harvey, and Robert Kaplan are exemplars of this approach.[15] In this perspective states are increasingly in conflict on traditional great power bases, but also on grounds of culture; international norms of security and civility are declining; at the same time, the state is increasingly unable within its domain to monopolize violence or control challenges to its authority. This is combined with the spread of weapons, nuclear and conventional, the explosion of the world's narcotics trade, the outbreak of warlordism and reckless violence and a globalized clamour of identity, community, whinging and vindictiveness of all stripes. For some this is a globalized trend, marked by the undermining of the state, and of state-based forms of order, in the contemporary world, for others it is specific to certain areas – the Balkans, OECD inner cities, Africa – where state authority and inter-state co-operation no longer operate. One consequence of this is the denial of international responsibilities with regard to peacekeeping and humanitarian protection: 'We cannot wipe the tear from every eye', in the words of one British MP, David Howell. 'Doing good is not a strategy' echoed the Republican Party foreign policy expert Condoleezza Rice. In such neo-medieval discourse, history is deployed to underline a pessimistic continuity that we ignore at our peril.

It would be precipitate to dismiss this perspective, a necessary and in some cases timely corrective to the complacency of those with power, and to the liberal optimism of some without. The Hobbesian cold eye never loses a certain relevance. Those who in developed societies are keen to renounce the state as the agent of repression would do well to spend some time in places like Somalia, Tajikistan or Lebanon where the state has, in recent years, been deficient. Yet this approach is in several respects misleading. First of all, we are a long way, in international relations or in domestic politics, from the Middle Ages. The state of today possesses a power and legitimacy far greater than anything seen centuries ago. Fanciful invocations of medieval private armies, and the *condottieri*, or of city states or multiple sovereignty, supposed to stress the similarity with the Middle Ages, are of limited analytic, or policy, relevance. The globalization of the economy alone marks us off from that period.

History is also a corrective in another way, for those who may be tempted to overstate the changes in the world since 1989: we hear much of the 'new nationalism', yet many of those nationalisms categorized as new – in Kurdistan, Germany, Ulster – are not that new. We hear much of warlordism – but Burma was rife with warlords during the cold war. The savagery of war is a scandal – but neither inequality of technological capability, nor attacks on civilians and crimes of gender, are specific to the modern period. When the British invaded Tibet in 1904, they had, at the decisive battle of Guru, about half a dozen non-fatal casualties, while the Tibetans lost between 600 and 700 dead, and another 168 wounded, out of a total force estimated at 1500.[16] The crimes against women in the Russian advance into eastern Europe in World War II or in the Indo-Pakistani War of 1947 dwarf any seen more recently in the Balkans. These problems do not gain urgency by being misdescribed as products of a new global anarchy.

Moreover, the retreat into explanation by atavism, a stock in trade of Robert Kaplan, or the recent political pronouncements of the novelist V.S. Naipaul, is equally misleading. For reasons discussed earlier, culture is not a constant or independent explanatory factor, but more a context, an idiom, in which changing priorities and interests express themselves. Equally, invocation of social Darwinist explanations of all, or some, state behaviour explain little, or nothing. The global pessimist also understates the room for purposeful action. For all the failings of international institutions in recent years, and indeed ever since 1945, they have shown a capacity for action, and intervention, that is far from the world of chaos conjured up by the protagonists of the 'New Middle Ages'. There is an internationalized concern, at state and non-state levels, with issues of justice and rights. There is a capacity, quite far developed, for handling global economic tensions. A startling idiom it may be, but a rigorous analytic approach the 'New Middle Ages' is not. The world at 2000 allows, perhaps, for no easy generalization: it does, however, pose a set of challenges that may come to dominate the decades ahead.

4

The Recurrence of War

Speculation about the new millennium has tended to stress a positive future, fuelled by economic prosperity and the Internet revolution. If it has expressed a note of concern, it has, above all, been about the inequality that is accompanying globalization and the prospect of this increasing. The perceptive *Financial Times* correspondent Martin Wolf wrote in one of his final columns of the last century that if there is one thing he would most wish to see in the future it would be the reduction in global inequality.[1] There is, however, one wish that is, arguably, even greater than that, and which takes precedence over all others, namely peace. The dangers of war, and the need to think clearly about them, have not disappeared from the world horizon. The world may be living on the edge of a new peaceful, globalized era without, at least, major conflicts between developed states. It may, however, be living in an 'Interregnum', a time when the dangers of war have receded, only to return later. The twentieth century has, among other perils, bequeathed to the twenty-first thousands of nuclear warheads, the means to deliver them, and the anxieties to continue deploying them. Outside the developed world, conflict, and preparation for it, continues and this may, in various ways, affect the developed world itself. A generation hence observers may look back contemptuously at the contemporary world as living in a fool's paradise, neglecting the causes of subsequent conflict and destruction. Carl von Clausewitz talked, rightly, of the 'fog of war' but it is also peace, with the complacency it generates and the hidden dangers it incubates, which generates its own fog of illusions, perhaps never more so than today.

War and Modernity

War, both in its international, that is, inter-state, form and in its internal, civil or inter-communal dimension, has been a formative influence in shaping the modern world: the map of the world as we know it, arbitrarily dividing territory and peoples, and invested with identities, histories and symbols of triumph and humiliation, is to a considerable degree a product of war. The development of the modern economy and state, of modern science and education, are also in large measure the product of the challenges of inter-state conflict. So too are the political systems that characterize modern societies: much as it may cause unease to admit it, the development of modern democracy is to a considerable degree a result of war, of the promises made to men, and women, by embattled elites in parts of Europe, of defeat in war, in the case of Germany and Japan, of the outcome of a bitter civil war and its political completion through the civil rights movement a hundred years later, in the case of America. Even as war itself has been transformed by industrialization, scientific advance and democratization, so too has it profoundly affected the world that produces it. War has, in this sense, been an intrinsic part of modernity and of the shaping of the politics, society and economics of the world as a whole.[2]

War has also been the first, and the classical, concern of the analysis of international relations: against the background of its centrality for the modern world, there have been two broad arguments about its place within the international system. One sees war as recurrent, a product, depending on theoretical position, of inter-capitalist competition; the tensions within society; the pressure of arms manufacturers and military officials; or the very multiplicity or 'anarchy' of states themselves. The contrary argument has been that war is, to an increasing degree, redundant in the modern world: the pastime of aristocrats in the eighteenth century, the resort of autocrats and dictators in the twentieth, it is, by dint of its destructive potential and the peaceful interests of industrialized societies, irrelevant to the modern world and the regulation of relations between states. The former argument is the favourite resort of, on the one hand, 'realists' and pessimists in international relations, quick to invoke the recurrence of history or – today reinforced by the rise of sociobiology – the effects of unchanging human nature. On the other hand, it is also the stock in trade of those, be they Marxists or others, who see modern capitalist society as inherently militaristic and aggressive. The latter argument was sketched by Immanuel Kant in the late eighteenth century, when he envisioned a world in which an increasingly constitutional and, implicitly, democratic politics within states would promote greater co-operation between them. In the nineteenth century and later sociologists examined the growing incompatibility of war with modern society. The belief in, and aspiration towards, a democratic *and* peaceful world were born.

The twentieth century lent support enough to both of these arguments: two world wars and the cold war, and many local conflicts, strengthened the belief in the recurrence of war; the growth of co-operation and peaceful resolution of disputes between developed democracies supported the latter. If this history of war has refuted any simple equation of modernity with peace, it does lend a partial, conditional support to the counter-argument: the case for a *necessary* relation between modernity and war has been seriously weakened, war appearing instead as a *contingent* product of modernizing society even as its utility, and the forces making for it, recede in relations between democratic developed states.

In the aftermath of the cold war the picture is, however, less clear now than at any moment in modern time. The world seems to be torn between two tendencies as regards war: a belief that the epoch of the great inter-state wars, as we have seen them from the eighteenth to the twentieth centuries, is over, and a concern that new forms of war, represented by the Balkans, central Africa and Colombia, are spreading. Many is the commentator and indeed philosopher who has speculated on this shift – the retreat from war in its classic form, the very 'debellicization' of modern society in the sense of decreased willingness to fight and to pay for military expenditure on the one hand – but alongside it the emergence of a virulent strand of internal war that lacks the controls, or the ideology, of earlier conflicts. The argument about contemporary war is linked to the broader speculation discussed in Chapter 1 about the changing nature of power itself – with economic power, even cultural and media power, displacing traditional military capability. Equally, contemporary discussion of war raises a question as to the ability of the developed, debellicized world to fulfil those security, and specifically peacekeeping, commitments, which the still bellicose world may pose for it: here, amidst other challenges, is the requirement which the 'modern' and 'pre-modern' pose to the 'post-modern' world.

There are reasons for not being entirely convinced by either of the main perspectives on war, that of 'debellicization' or that of 'new' wars, and for drawing little comfort from each. Military power always had limits, and was never the sole or in many cases most efficacious means by which states achieved their goals. Yet, as discussed in Chapter 1, it has continued to be used to political purpose in the modern world. War is also an instrument for the rectification of wrongs – all moral orders allow for the right to revolt. At the same time military capability remains essential to the running of any overall global system – to maintain peace within and between states, to guarantee the security and regulation of an international economic order and, where just, to implement the will of the international community against aggressors, within and between states. If only because the use of force remains an issue for all states, the political, and moral, issues inherent in the use of military forces have not, and will not, go away. If we look at the dangers of inter-state war, then it is certainly the case that, *in the form in which the last century knew them*, major inter-state military competitions have receded from parts of the world, particularly Europe. The candidates for causing world wars, be they 1914, 1939 or the crises of the cold war, are not, on present evidence, heading for a confrontation: put in global terms, the Europeans are, for the foreseeable future, behaving themselves. Most obviously, the Balkans are not an international powder keg as they were in the first two decades of the twentieth century. Germany is not a restless power and it and the other western European states are embedded in the EU and NATO. Russia, for all its criticism of the west, is not for a generation at least able, or willing, to enter a serious strategic competition again. Some years from now, even that could change, and the mood of resentment in Russia, which so underpinned popular support for the criminal war in Chechnya, could indeed provoke a new militarization. But this is not a proximate, or inevitable, danger. To identify the sources of conflict we need to look elsewhere, at shifts in the pattern of warfare itself, and at those regions of the world where the prospect of inter-state war persists.

The Evolution of Insecurity

If the period since the end of the cold war has indeed marked a significant reduction in the core global military conflict, that between the

NATO alliance and the ex-Soviet bloc, it has, however, been accompanied by other trends that increase both the incidence of war and its likelihood in the future. First, the period since 1991 has been one in which several dozen wars have broken out or continued despite changed international circumstances.[3] As was the case in the cold war, many of these have been wars involving ethnic conflict or demands for secession. What has been different, however, has been the re-emergence of wars of this kind in Europe, for the first time since World War II, and their increasing enmeshing with forms of organized criminality and economic interest. A feature of these wars has been the ability of rebel groups to sustain themselves by transnational economic activities – raising money from diasporas (KLA, Tamil Tigers, PKK, IRA), trading in raw materials and precious metals produced in their own areas (Cambodia, Angola, Sierra Leone), or producing and refining narcotics (Colombia). In many cases the actors involved, be they states or rebel groups, have engaged in widespread and systematic violations of the rules of war, against civilians, women, children and prisoners. For some this betokens a 'new' kind of war, if not a new phase in international relations facilitated by a more permissive international context than the cold war in which revolutionary and counter-revolutionary wars were either armed or constrained by the USA and the Soviet Union.[4]

Yet, as discussed in Chapter 3, it may be mistaken to see these conflicts as marking a fundamentally new phase of warfare, or world politics. Nor would it seem that this kind of warfare is a wave of the future: in Europe, the terrible wars of the 1990s have given way to a cold, but in large measure effective, peace. In Latin America, Colombia is a unique case, building on a history of conflict that goes back to the 1940s, in some respects to the nineteenth century: the main guerrilla groups, the FARC and ELN, are very much products of the cold war, of the radical guerrilla movement that swept Latin America in the 1960s and 70s. It is in Africa that the incidence of war is most striking: but here it reflects, as much as ethnic or intra-state conflict, the vitality of rivalries between states – whether in a straight inter-state war, as between Ethiopia and Eritrea, or in the internationalized civil wars of Zaire and Angola.

Terrorism, in what is termed its 'international' form, constitutes a second issue that is seen as promoting insecurity in the contemporary world. By terrorism is conventionally meant the use of violence, against civilians, by opposition forces either within a domestic context or internationally. The last decades of the twentieth century saw numerous terrorist incidents of this kind. In 1998 two US embassies in East Africa were blown up, an action that led to Washington firing cruise missiles against targets in Afghanistan (where the originators of the blasts probably did have base facilities) and Sudan (where they probably did not). There is no reason to believe that such actions will not recur: hence a literature, parallel to that on 'new wars', of 'new terrorism'.

Yet an element of proportion is essential here. First, terrorist acts of this kind, what we may term 'terrorism from below', have been endemic in modern society for over a century. Terrorism, like torture, is in large measure a product of modern society, its ideologies and political movements: yet it is not noticeably *more* frequent in the post-1989 world than before. Second, it is a mistake to focus only on actions by rebels involved in conflict against states. The great mass of criminal activities against civilians and others are carried out not by rebel groups, but by states: this sense of 'terrorism', the original usage since the time of the French Revolution, remains prevalent in much of the world. Third, the great majority of acts of 'terrorism from below' are committed not against other states, let alone those of the west, but in situations of inter-communal conflict: this was long the case in Sri Lanka, Kashmir, Lebanon, and became so again in the 1990s in Rwanda, Bosnia and Sierra Leone. It is neighbouring communities, not the enemy far afield, that are the primary target of terrorist acts: 'national' terrorism is a far greater concern, and crime, than its 'international' counterpart. Finally, terrorism has not, in recent times, become a major *international* phenomenon, in the sense of either provoking inter-state conflict (as it did at Sarajevo in 1914) or seriously challenging the workings of the international system. It is dramatic, cruel, sudden but not, on the record of the last part of the twentieth century, a challenge to global order. Threat inflation with regard to terrorism, as with regard to nuclear weapons, is another pernicious legacy of cold war.

A third trend in global insecurity is the spread of what are termed 'Weapons of Mass Destruction' (WMD) – nuclear, chemical and biological weapons. These have existed for much of the twentieth century: chemical weapons were used in World War I and later by Arab states, nuclear in World War II. The dream, and fear, of a 'super-weapon', which would assure absolute mastery of the world haunted a century bemused by science fiction. The reality turned out to be somewhat less dramatic: the major cold war powers constructed and stored such weapons, yet they did not use them, or pass them on to third parties. Nuclear non-proliferation was a successful rule of the cold war – leading, in the case of the USSR's relationship with China, to a major breach in 1960–63. Terrible crimes were committed in the twentieth century: mass bombing of civilians was the most evident example. But the most terrible of these were carried out in large measure with the instruments of earlier times – murder chambers and gas ovens, firing squads, knives and machetes. It was political will, and an inhuman respect for orders and community, that caused mass destruction, not the products of science.

The period since the early 1990s has seen some unravelling of this. Several states, that previously did not have nuclear potential, have now either acquired nuclear weapons, or are evidently able to do so. Controls on fissile material, means of delivery and on scientific personnel associated with the cold war were eroded. As the case of Iraq showed, it was possible for a committed state to acquire WMD of all three kinds without the knowledge of international observers, and, as was shown in its war with Iran from 1980 to 1988, to use chemical weapons, and stockpile large numbers of biological weapons, without sanction. It was not scientific change that yielded this: it was political will to use, combined with international reluctance to prevent, that marked a dangerous new turning point.

The proliferation of WMD, however, cannot be extrapolated in a direct and simple way to the proposition that we live in a more dangerous world. States, and their leaders, may have conflicting goals but they are generally not irrational. Even Saddam Hussein showed a cold, and effective, calculation in his occupation and withdrawal from Kuwait: if he gambled, wrongly, that the world would let him stay in Kuwait, he was right in estimating that, once he had withdrawn, his hold on power in Iraq itself would not be seriously threatened. The spread of WMD is in large, although not sole, measure a result of anxiety among states about the threat of others, rather than a token of an aggressive intent. In many cases, a political, diplomatic solution to the issues that underlie insecurity could be explored. Although the opponents of neither would welcome the comparison, both Israel and Iran have pursued WMD programmes in order to deter the threat of attack, a real enough prospect in the light of recent history. The North Korean programme was, equally, rooted in the failure to find a political solution to the problems of the peninsula. The exceptions were Iraq and the South-east Asian states, India and Pakistan. Here the allure of political advantage, not rational calculations of insecurity, triggered a process of weapons acquisition. It was in these areas, among others, that the danger of inter-state war persisted. An undifferentiated anxiety may be avoided, but a geographically specific one may not.

The Prospect of Inter-state War

In the European and American continents the realm of insecurity has been radically reduced. The situation is very different in other areas of the world, where inter-state rivalry has not receded with the end of the cold war and where new forms of weaponry, particularly in regard to missiles and weapons of mass destruction, provide states with new opportunities for military action. Three notable such areas are the Far East, South Asia and the Persian Gulf. Ominously, none has been a stranger to war in modern times.

The first shots of what were to be the great inter-state wars of the twentieth century were fired in 1894–95 in the first Sino-Japanese War. The region was the scene of terrible destruction in World Wars I and II, in the latter case involving the use of nuclear weapons. During the cold war, the bloodiest conflicts by far were in East Asia – the Chinese revolution, and the Korean and Vietnam Wars. Today the region is the scene of great economic growth and prosperity, but it would be naive to assume that this and economic interdependence alone will necessarily stay the hand of war. States, and peoples, are capable of getting into war even if it does cause great economic damage. In China we see the rise of a new sentiment of nationalism, linked to a sense of past grievance against the west and Japan, and fuelled by the crisis in the hitherto dominant ideology of Marxism. Inevitably as the hold of communism fades it will be replaced by other mechanisms of control and manipulation – by corruption and connections instead of party discipline, and by nationalism instead of the thoughts of Marx, Lenin and Mao Zedong. The institution which is gradually replacing the party as the mainstay of the regime is the army.

The dangers in China's relations with other states arise in three directions. First, there is the question of Taiwan. China has said it will go to war if Taiwan declares independence, and it is increasingly able to inflict damage on that country without mounting the mass amphibious operation across the 160 miles of the Taiwan straits that it has neither the capability for domination in the air nor the transport capacity to mount. Although small – an estimated 18 CSS-4 strategic missiles and 60 CSS-2,3,5 intermediate missiles – China's capability in this field and that of satellites may give it the ability not only to hit targets on Taiwan but also to locate, and threaten, any US or Japanese ships that might be sent to Taiwan's support. Second, there is the unresolved issue of Korea: North Korea is in a precarious condition, and too little is known about the strategic calculations of its political leadership. It could continue in this state for many a year yet. Equally it could implode, as a result of factionalism within the regime. Sooner or later, it will go the way of other countries divided in the cold war and now absorbed by their stronger capitalist counterparts, Germany and Yemen. A situation of uncertainty, or violence, accompanying the transition in North Korea could have serious regional consequences. Third, there are the disputed islands of the South China seas, claimed by Vietnam, China and other states: small islands do not cause wars, but they can act as the spark for war in situations where underlying conflicts and pressures, strategic and political, are building up.

South Asia represents a second zone of potential inter-state conflict.[5] India and Pakistan have already fought three wars: in 1947, 1965 and 1971. The province of Kashmir, partitioned between them, remains not only in dispute but the scene of recurrent violence for which both states must bear responsibility. In both India and Pakistan, there are also strong nationalist and confrontational forces at work. In India, the 1990s have seen the rise of a Hindu nationalism espousing a militaristic view of Hindu culture and threatening non-Hindus inside India as well as, on occasion, calling for the liquidation of Pakistan itself. In Pakistan, growing fragmentation and violence within the country has been fuelled by Islamic fundamentalists, drug dealers and political corruption.[6] The prime responsibility for the worsening of this situation must lie with India, which in May 1998 exploded a nuclear bomb and led Pakistan to follow suit. The reasons given for India's nuclear breakout were threadbare in the extreme: much was made of a supposed but in reality non-existent Chinese threat; another common notion was that India had to make up for centuries, or millennia, of wrongs committed by outsiders – an argument which could, of course, be made by every country in the world.

Wise souls, and those who believe nuclear weapons stabilize the world, argue that nuclear deterrence can stabilize South Asia. This is, certainly, fondly to be desired. But there are reasons for doubting that this will be the case. First of all, stable deterrence requires firm, established, political authority in the countries concerned: this does not apply, and on present form will not in the foreseeable future, to either India or Pakistan. What we see instead is a competition for factional, communal and party advantage that is internationally destabilizing as far as the conduct of foreign and defence policy is concerned. Second, the nuclear peace that reigned in Europe during the cold war had the benefit of a significant 'buffer zone' between the main protagonists – Russia in the east, France, Britain and the USA in the west. No such space exists in South Asia, where India and Pakistan are next-door neighbours. Third, the nuclear peace in Europe was reinforced by the dampening effect of the 'Iron Curtain', a humanitarian crime, but also a guarantee against sudden crises and unexpected escalations. In South Asia, by contrast, there is the contested area of Kashmir, which Pakistan seeks to destabilize and India refuses to conciliate: the majority of the inhabitants, themselves of diverse linguistic and religious character, want neither direct rule by India nor absorption by Pakistan. They are, however, the victims of inter-state rivalry and self-proclaimed liberators.

The third great area of instability is the Persian Gulf. Here too there has been a history of war – no less, by my count, than three inter-state 'Gulf Wars'. The first, between Iran and Iraq, lasted from 1969 to 1975: it ended with the Algiers Accord of 1975, which delimited the boundary between these states and committed them to non-interference in each other's internal affairs. That was a reasonable deal, which could have formed the basis for a general reduction of tensions in the area. But it was destroyed by the Iranian Revolution of 1979, which led to renewed interference by Iran and Iraq in each other's affairs, and, after months of border incidents and mutual abuse, to the start of the second Gulf War, when Saddam Hussein invaded Iran in September 1980. That war lasted until August 1988 and cost hundreds of thousands of lives: it was the second longest inter-state war of the twentieth century after the Sino-Japanese War of 1937–45, which lasted two months longer. What is more, the failure of Iraq to defeat Iran and to impose its terms on the post-Khomeini leadership in Tehran led directly to the third Gulf War of

1990: with nothing to show for eight years of war with Iran, Saddam Hussein sought compensation elsewhere and invaded Kuwait.

In one sense, all of this conflict in the Gulf was, and is, avoidable. None of the issues in dispute in the Gulf is intractable, there are no major boundary disputes. Iran and the Emirates contest some small islands, but these are hardly inhabited: they occasion, as the Argentinian writer Jorge Luis Borges said of the British and the Argentinians over the Falklands, 'a fight between two bald men over a comb'.[7] The sources of conflict lie *within* the countries themselves, and in particular in the way in which modern nationalism has constructed a competition and division that has drawn them into war. It could do so again. The basis of any security system in the Gulf is the triangle of the three most powerful states – Iran, Iraq, Saudi Arabia. Until and unless all three have minimal co-operative relations with each other, there is the danger of further conflict. At the moment external forces keep a precarious peace, but there is no guaranteeing how long they will stay. Iraq, meanwhile, is regaining confidence and freedom of manoeuvre. What Saddam has tried twice before, invading Iran and then Kuwait, he could do again.

The 'Revolution in Military Affairs'

It is not only the practice but also the theory of war which have changed since the end of the cold war. One dimension of this, a direct result of the conflicts which broke out during the 1990s, has been the development of new conceptions of peacekeeping and peace-enforcement, and of an intermediate domain, sometimes known as 'peacemaking' or 'Chapter Six and a Half', in reference to the UN Charter. All armies participating in UN and other humanitarian operations have faced considerable challenges in adapting to the new complexities of involvement in conflict situations, where enforcing peace, fighting violations of that peace and providing aid and assistance to the civilian population may intertwine.

Yet this development in the political and low-level tactics of military activity has been combined with something very different, the emergence of a new conception of warfare, pioneered in the USA, that would allow for greater superiority in war than seen in modern inter-state contexts. Sometimes termed the 'Revolution in Military Affairs' (RMA), it has two broad components: one a much more rapid, integrated system of battlefield command and control, the other the use of precision missiles and bombs to allow for long-range assaults on enemy targets.[8] Both were enabled by the technological advances which the USA alone was making, both allowed for the spectre of a war in which combat troops would not be used, and in which casualties would be minimal. If the Gulf War of 1991 gave some inkling of this, the aerial campaigns against Iraq in the late 1990s, and against Serbian targets in both 1995 and 1999, were a small realization of this potential. The prospect of a National Missile Defence (NMD) system in the USA is but one further potential chapter in the realization of this programme, using technological superiority to ensure victory.

The political consequences of this RMA are, potentially, enormous. On the one hand, they place the USA in a position of unchallenged superiority, not only vis-à-vis potential foes, most obviously Russia and China, but also serve to highlight the gap between the US capability and that of its allies. The Europeans were not capable of the 'intelligence superiority' which this shift in technology made possible. Yet the RMA itself raises as many questions as it answers. First, it is not at all clear how seriously to take some of the claims made for new technology in the military sphere: the case for NMD rests, for example, on widely contested tests and probabilities of detection and accuracy. NMD would also be susceptible to such countermeasures as large-scale use of decoys. What is more, today's new technologies associated with computerization were, above all, designed for the civilian sector: the most modern technology was not, as it had been in the immediate post-1945 decades, in military equipment but in the high street computer store. Second, air superiority has not been, on its own, sufficient to achieve political goals: it could pound, or deter, a potential foe, but it was of no use in situations of civil conflict.

The most ominous question of all, however, concerns the political implications of the RMA and the increased tensions between the USA and its allies occasioned by the NMD and by, what is now considered to be the centre of any twenty-first century military strategy, superiority in information and intelligence. In effect, NMD and 'intelligence superiority' run the risk of decoupling US defence from what for many, especially the Republican right, had been an unusual, transitory commitment to the security of European states. NMD, presented as a system of around 100 interceptors based in

Alaska, would in no conceivable way be a means of removing Russia's attack capability. It is, however, implausible that such a system was going to be deployed at the cost of $30 billion over ten years just to deal with North Korea and Iran: the former could be deterred by other means and might well disappear, the latter would cease to be a strategic threat once the Lebanese and Palestinian issues had entered a new phase. Between these small threats, and that of Russia, there lies, however, the largely unspoken one, that of China, the enemy that is both credible and long-standing, if the Taiwan issue is not resolved. Here polls indicate that an over-whelming majority of US public opinion favours deploying NMD.

Precisely because it highlights the capability gap between the USA and all other states, and because of the lack of credibility of its claimed strategic purpose, NMD runs the risk of increasing global resentment and suspicion of what the USA intends. It is in its political and ideological effects, not its lethal potential, that lies the greatest cost of the RMA. It is most certainly not an auspicious note on which to commence a new era of global peace.

Possibilities of Peace

Assessment of the risks of war is not in the end a matter of predicting the inevitable or recognizing the fated, but rather of re-emphasizing the fundamental link between war and politics: politics, which cause war, can equally be used to prevent it. No one contemplating the world at 2000 could be confident that the era of international peace, the final redundancy of war and attainment of democratic peace, was at hand. Just as the twentieth century had begun with local wars that presaged a century of conflict to come, with mass mobilization for insurrection in China and Boer guerrilla war in South Africa, so the twenty-first began amidst the still smouldering ashes of Kosovo, the ongoing brutalities of Chechnya, inter-state confrontation between Ethiopia and Eritrea to name but some.

These were not inevitable conflicts, nor did they reflect the return of some innate, 'tribal' or atavistic behaviour: they were, in origin and course, products of the contemporary world, fought with contemporary means and for contemporary ends. Each of these conflicts allowed, in abstract, for political resolution: the disputes between states could be solved by compromise and mediation, those within by the forging of coalition governments. While many conflicts had evaded settlement, the last decade of the twentieth century had, indeed, seen several cases of negotiated settlements between, and within, states – in Namibia, South Africa, El Salvador, Nicaragua, Cambodia – and in the launching of at least partially successful peace processes in Ireland, Lebanon, and Israel/Palestine. Negotiation, international peacekeeping, financial commitments and good luck all contributed to these outcomes, and, of no small significance, to sustaining the momentum of negotiation once this had started.

Diplomacy is not, however, enough. The most hopeful prospect for a peaceful world at the dawn of the twenty-first century lay in the consolidation and extension of the zone of democratic peace, encompassing the main regions of Europe, and North America, and the bringing of other regions of the world into this system of economic development and democratic government. In the longer run, of course, it would be foolish to discount the possibility of an unravelling of that zone: the very contingency of the relationship between modernity and war contains within it the possibility of another phase of world history in which the major industrialized states, resiling from an imperfect but nonetheless substantial democracy, may resort once again to war. However, in the intermediate/conjunctural timescale of the foreseeable decades that would seem to be less likely than the prospect of war between undemocratic states, or that between the democratic and the undemocratic.

In this context it is unsurprising that the notion of a 'democratic peace' has become increasingly influential despite the fact that its own democratic heartlands themselves emerged from centuries of war, had – whether democratic or not – visited war on others, and retained institutions, and cultures, that are in many respects profoundly illiberal and prone to discount external responsibilities. Yet the association of peace with prosperity and democracy is not trivial, and suggests how, beyond the impact of diplomacy and the maintenance of peace, the aspiration to a more peaceful world could be realized. The implication is, therefore, clear: a peaceful world requires one in which economic well-being and political freedom are more broadly realized. These constitute, therefore, the two other major challenges of the new era.

5

Globalization and its Discontents

Definition and History

Globalization has become from the early 1990s onwards the central topic of debate in social science and in much public debate, in both developed and developing societies. That *something* momentous and far-reaching is going on is indisputable even if its likely end state is not yet possible to discern. There is, however, a need, in the bacchanalian whirl of generalization and meta-historical claim which has masked discussion of globalization, for conceptual precision both about *what* the term is supposed to mean and about *what it is* that is being globalized. More caution than has often been evident is also required about mixing into one supposedly unified process what are often distinct developments, to leave open how far the different elements of globalization are indeed connected. Changes in family structure, or the rise and fall of secular ideas, or the spread of fast food, are not necessarily related to trade liberalization or the Internet; the collapse of communism was only partially related to the processes known as globalization, even though the two processes coincided in the late 1980s and early 1990s; the rise of ethnic and nationalist protest movements, and the cult of identity, may be seen equally as a revolt *against* globalization *and* a component of it.

It is also rather important to probe the term 'global' itself: not everyone who travels abroad, or every firm that exports a percentage of their product, is global in a significant degree; many of the processes associated with globalization are largely confined to a few societies or economies – more regional than global, with large sections of the world almost entirely excluded. The term 'globalization' covers, therefore, a multiple of processes and the world might be better off it had not been used: it is fuzzier than the 'state' or 'economy', themselves no exemplars of precision, up with 'nation' 'power' and 'structure' in the league table of social science imprecision.[1]

At its simplest, globalization denotes three things: a marked *reduction in the barriers* between societies and states, an *increasing homogeneity* of societies and states and an *increase in the volume of interactions* between societies – be this in terms of trade, capital, volumes of currency traded or movements of tourists and migrants. In the field of economics, this means trade liberalization and the increased tendency of capital to flow across frontiers: global trade in goods and services rose nearly threefold between the 1970s and 1997; foreign direct investment rose sevenfold to $400 billion in the same period; the daily turnover in foreign exchange markets rose from around $15 billion in 1973 to $1.5 trillion in 1998.[2] This was greatly facilitated by the fall in the costs of communication: airline operating costs fell by 50% between 1960 and 1990; sea-freight facilities have been greatly enhanced through containerization; the price of computers has fallen from thousands of dollars to a few hundred or less: 'the average cost of processing information fell from $75 per million operations to less than a hundredth of a cent' in the same period.[3] In political terms globalization means greater co-ordination between governments and at the same time greater interaction of non-governmental groups across frontiers. Discussion of globalization often emphasizes the increased power of multi-national corporations as against states. In cultural terms it means an increased interaction of cultures, beyond the control of states or established cultural authorities. Not least, globalization is associated with the technological revolution and the Internet. Some writers make broader claims about the relationship between these increased transactions between societies and shifting conceptions associated with a 'post-modern' world marked by new inter-relationships of space, time, identity: here scepticism is in order.

Such definition gets the argument some way, but there remains widespread scope for imprecision. Even if globalization is defined in economic terms, the definition may range from ratios of exports to GDP, through measures of trade and investment liberalization, to calculations of ratios of inward to outward investment. Political correlates cover both the role of states and the growing activity of the 'non-state'.

Discussion of multinational corporations needs similar precision: first, the criteria for what it is to be a multinational need to be specified – exporting to a range of countries does not of itself make a firm 'multinational'[4]; second, there are still very few firms that do not have a clear state, or 'national', identification in terms of location of headquarters and primacy of political relations; third, when it comes to the underpinnings of globalization – security, regulation, legal framework for business – it remains states which are essential. In weak, developing societies multinationals can in large measure evade state control: but the majority of investment, employment and trade by multinationals is in developed societies where the rule of law and the power of the state are considerable. Here any simple association of multinationals with globalization is unfounded: it is the states who through legislation and international co-operation are driving globalization, sometimes against the wishes of the multinationals themselves.

If definition is one requirement of a focused discussion on globalization, historical perspective is the other. While the term itself is associated with the late twentieth century, much of what is discussed today under the rubric of 'globalization' has been taking place for decades, if not centuries: the incorporation of the world into a single capitalist economic system began half a millennium before, around 1500; the movement of ideas, people, religious, cultural and political forces across frontiers has equally taken place for centuries. In part, globalization seems newer than it is because these processes were restricted and controlled by the risk of a powerful modern state and of the value system subsumed in nationalism: these sought to divide the world up into separate linguistic and cultural, and at the same time homogeneous, entities. Globalization could be said to represent, in this sense, the end of a detour associated with state attempts to protect the domestic economy and to build mutually exclusive productive and trading areas. Yet it is in large measure driven by states and is to an increasing degree requiring different forms of inter-state regulation.

A historical perspective backwards may, however, also invite a look into the future, raising the question not so much *when* and how will globalization end, but *on the basis of what criteria* might we judge that it has ended. A complete fusion of state, cultures, languages, peoples is neither feasible nor desirable. What is desirable and, arguably, feasible is that the enormous differences in access to wealth and the good life associated with the modern world should be overcome: here globalization invites a challenge that goes right to the heart of its record to date. The issue that is most significant for the direction of the world at the start of the twenty-first century is equality: the current process of globalization is a profoundly unequal and destabilizing one. Even if, in the economic sphere, the growing integration of economies creates greater opportunities for some, it also leaves each society liable to the fluctuations of others.

In political terms, the onset of a new phase of international cooperation is also the opportunity for great vulnerability. Herein lie the great challenges posed by globalization in each of the areas that it affects. Here too the link to the end of the cold war is clearer, and more exigent, than might at first sight appear: far from great strategic and ideological rivalries having ended the debate on globalization and its motor, capitalism, the shift in world politics at the end of the twentieth century has opened up capitalism to much greater scrutiny. Prior to the twentieth century, the processes of industrialization and modernization were confined to a small part of the world: the challenge was to meet expectations within these societies. For most of the twentieth century the capitalist world had an alibi, a claim that, whatever its faults, it was superior to its rival, communism. The non-western world has now been incorporated into the economic and political system of the west: the competition of the cold war has been won. Now capitalism has to be matched against the claims that it makes for itself. Capitalism is on its own. For the first time in history it lacks an alibi.

Instabilities and Inequalities

Globalization may, therefore, be seen as the second great challenge facing the world today, this challenge being understood in a double sense, to encompass not only the *effects* of the social and economic processes that comprise globalization, but also globalization's *ability to distribute* the benefits that modern society produces across the world.

The question of effects raises, first, the issue of how far the boom of the 1990s can be sustained, and how far, in broader terms, a new phase of capitalism, driven above all by the communications revolution, is at hand. There is a tendency, and more than that, in much current coverage of globalization to assume that the major economic problems of the world have been solved, that all we need is more of the same. In some fundamental respects this is not so. Historically the most persistent instability of all is that of productive and growth cycles, a feature of the modern capitalist system for more than a century and a half. We can have no way of knowing if this historical pattern of cyclical instability is over. It may conceivably be, but it is far from evident that this is so. The fate of the Japanese economy throughout the 1990s, in which neither government policy moves nor the increasing desperation of the private sector was able to reverse stagnation, speaks for itself. Between 1990 and 1999, Japan's gross public debt rose from 69% to 128% of GDP, and is expected to rise to 150% by 2004, while GDP growth lay at under 1% on average. Concern about cycles is not a prerogative of Marxists, or the followers of Kondratieff: the works of some leading contemporary economists point to an underlying concern that the current boom could end.[5] The US boom of the 1990s was based on consumer spending and business investment, fuelled by private sector debt. Borrowing was increased by rising house prices and stock market levels – both bubbles could, and may well, burst. Such a crisis could well call into question one of the underlying principles of globalization, the reduced role of the state: it remains to be seen to what extent a recession in the USA will lead that other erstwhile partner in economic management, the state, to step in to redress the balance. It is, therefore, far too early to argue for a fundamentally 'new' phase of capitalism, either in terms of the engines of growth, or in terms of a secular overcoming of the cycles that have hitherto beset the system. As more than a few cases in the 1990s illustrated, anyone who thinks they have, once and for all, cracked the secret of how productive cycles operate is likely to be confounded.

If the end of cycles within production is an open question, there are three other trends that are more visible, which relate to the patterns of distribution of wealth and opportunity within globalization and which have more certain negative effects. The first is employment. For much of the past 200 years there has been a trend, above all through industrialization, technological and economic growth, towards increased employment. This has been the motor of urbanization and migration. In the post-1945 world, 'full employment', variously defined, became a universal aspiration. But that link between economic growth and employment may now be under threat. Not only is there, as a result of technological change, a decline in the two most important historical forms of employment, agriculture and industry, but the changing relationship between technological change and employment quite simply means that the world does not need the labour force that exists. The next phase in production organization, and indeed in parts of the service sector, is robotization, a process that may challenge many hitherto secure areas of employment in developed economies: a combination of Internet purchasing of goods, and robotization of retail warehouses, threatens to transform urban life. Throughout the world economy, this gap between labour supply and demand is accompanied by a growing insecurity or casualization of employment. This process is all the more a problem because of two other related trends – the demographic explosion on the one hand, the rising aspirations of people worldwide on the other. For some parts of the developed world – Europe, Japan – the problem will be of a labour shortage. But this is not the issue worldwide.

Global demographic trends mean that the world has to create 30 million new jobs every year until 2050. According to the International Labour Organization, around one-third of the world's labour force, or one billion people, are already unemployed or underemployed. Job creation, by fair means or foul, is therefore becoming *the* major challenge of the twenty-first century, both for the general pattern of north–south relations and within many countries. It underlies both political instability in many states, and the reluctance of states to withdraw from inefficient job-creation schemes, but also the worldwide pressure for migration, both within and between states. At some point in the 1980s, the world passed another epochal transition point as, for the first time, the majority of the world's population came to live in urban areas. In 1975, 60% of the world's population lived in rural areas; in 2000 this had fallen to just over 40%.[6] The cities of the developing world are exploding. At the same time millions seek to reach the more developed states. Providing employment and maintaining its security are the economic tasks which the current phase of scientific and technological change does least to address.

A second trend intrinsic to the current organization of the world economy, although not arguably to capitalism itself, is the growing instability of financial and currency markets.[7] The indices of a global financial instability are there: in the past decade there have been significant banking crises in over 125 countries. The USA itself has seen more than one crisis in major financial institutions. The IT revolution has encouraged an over-stimulation of stocks that itself leads to greater market swings. This is exacerbated by the very increase in the volumes of money traded, the weaknesses of financial institutions in many countries and the very irrationality and insecurity of speculative frenzy. The last involves something too easily taken as 'natural', the spectacle replicated day after day in the global casino of grown men and women screaming into their mobiles and at their screens as they play for the shortest of short-term benefits with the welfare of billions of people, a frenzy now accentuated by the communications revolution. Since so much of market activity is ruled by a self-generated psychology, excitement can quickly crash.

The greatest insecurity in the world economy is, however, born of global, and rising, inequality: herein lies the delusion suggested by the very term 'globalization' itself. The world has always been, but is increasingly, controlled by a minority of states and economies, that is, it is oligarchic. If the Industrial Revolution, and the creation of a single world economy, laid the foundations of this inequality, the long post-1945 boom up to the mid-1970s, and now neo-liberal globalization, have accentuated it. The processes intrinsic to globalization are not distributed globally. Foreign direct investment (FDI) totalled $400 in 1997, yet close on 60% of this went to OECD states; of the remainder, over 80% went to just 20 countries – the greatest beneficiary, China, receiving $45 billion: three times more than the next nearest recipient, Brazil. For over 100 countries, FDI averaged less than $100 million a year.

The overall record of the twentieth century in terms of the distribution of wealth, laid out in the 1999 UNDP *Human Development Report*, speaks for itself. The income gap between the richest fifth of the world's population and the poorest fifth stood at around 3:1 in 1820, 11:1 in 1913, 30:1 in 1970, 60:1 in 1990 and 86:1 at the century's end. By 1997, the top 20% of the global population living in high-income countries earned 86% of world GDP, the middle 60% earned 13% and the bottom 20% just 1%. This inequality in per capita income is replicated in other indexes: the top 20% account for 82% of international trade and 68% of FDI.

The relative figures could, of course, be tempered by the argument that even as the gap widens, the overall level of income and well-being, however measured, is increasing: this is a classical counter-argument of liberal economics. Growth has been diffused across much of the globe, and with it a rise in living standards and life expectancy. Those who see national economies, or the world economy, as a zero-sum game are wrong. Increasing wealth for some does not necessarily entail increasing poverty for others. But the facts are not so comforting. First, over a third of the world's countries, 80 out of 195, have lower per capita incomes at the end of the 1990s than a decade before. This is the scale of the limits on a global trickle-down. Second, this fall corresponds to the fact that almost a quarter of the world's population, 1.3 billion people according to the UNDP, have daily incomes of under one US dollar and half under two dollars. Third, the life conditions of many are further reduced by the plagues of the modern world – the spread of AIDS especially to large sections of the population in parts of Africa, environmental degradation, and the squalor of rapidly growing cities.

Even the relative figures would, in themselves, be enough to cause great concern – on ethical and practical grounds. As suggested in Chapter 3, a world of such growing inequality, and an inequality that is universally perceived as such, will not be a stable one: pressures to control natural resources, competition for advantage, and above all massive pressure to migrate will and do result from such perceived differences. There is a clear link too between the incidence of intra-state wars, with their terrible human and transnational consequences, and poverty. Rich citizenries may go to war with each other, but they are certainly less likely to do so than poor and resentful ones. In terms of mass perception, it is far too easily forgotten, in the developed world, just how much resentment the current development of the world economy creates. Globalization is not seen as a wonderful advantage, but as another hegemonic project, teleguided by the rich and powerful, to subjugate and exploit the poorer and weaker majority of the world. Conspiracy theories abound about how satellite television, or the IT revolution, or changes in international trade and finance are manipulated to suit the global elite. The key arguments about international politics, and international justice, in the twenty-first century will, to a considerable degree, be about the terms in which globalization is realized.

Scientific and Technological Change

The social and political challenge of globalization, however, is not only one of economic benefits, in employment and income terms, but also of the pattern of distribution of the scientific achievements that benefit the developed world.

Surveys of the world produced around the time of the millennium paid particular attention to what was happening in this sphere, not least because of the argument derived from economic history as to technology being the main stimulant of growth.[8] On the optimistic side, there are the enormous changes in information technology and in the life sciences. The IT revolution is continuing, growing apace and knows no limits: Internet usage is increasing at 80% per month, the impact of which on the conduct and very character of the economy, as on education and the media, is enormous. Everyday lives, not least interpersonal relations, are being profoundly affected. Those born into this age have a radically different view of knowledge, and earning an income, from those of an earlier time. One striking example is the empowerment of older people, often women, who can use e-mail to keep in touch regularly, and without all the hassles and psychological stresses associated with the phone.

On the negative side, we face the continued and unresolved issue of the environment. Leaving aside the more alarmist projections, it is evident that something very profound is happening to the world's climate and that human activity is playing a major role in it. The temperature of the world rose by 1°F between 1900 and 2000. Responsible predictions now suggest a rise of 3–6°F by 2100. This is not only continuing but is largely unchecked. The Conventions of Montreal, Rio de Janeiro and Kyoto have reflected some willingness to deal with the issue of climate change. But the major underlying trends, which relate to production and consumption patterns, are not being confronted. No state in the world has taken decisive measures to curb the use of motor transport: the trend of modern life is more and more towards it. A society that is willing to ban cigarette advertisements would not do the same in relation to what is arguably a greater threat, the sale of motor cars. When a society treats car advertisements in the same way it treats those of cigarettes, this may be an index of resolve. Oil-producing states lobby hard against what they see as discriminatory carbon taxes in the rich economies. The destruction of the world's forests continues. The oceans, and the upper atmosphere, are dumping grounds for human waste products. The world of 2100 may be one without fish.

To these changes in the environment must be added the spread of new forms of disease, most notably that of AIDS and, more broadly, the collapse in forms of public health that had accounted for so much of the improvement in the previous century. By 1 January 2000 over

16 million people had already died of AIDS, 14 million of them in sub-Saharan Africa. There are an estimated 33 million people around the world living with HIV, the virus that causes AIDS: of these 90% are believed to be unaware of their infection. The spread of the disease at epidemic levels to India and East Asia is believed to be in prospect. For some countries in the world, most notably Africa, the incidence of AIDS has reached a point where it may overwhelm the society as a whole – both in terms of the costs of treatment and the longer-run depletion of the labour force.

In regard to health, as on the environment, public concern oscillates between alarm and denial. The epidemiological evidence on the prospects for the next generation, or even over the next decade, is alarming. The World Health Organization has warned of a collapse in global health levels, as microbes become more and more resistant to antibiotics: the return of typhoid in India; the spread of tuberculosis in former communist states; the resistance of gonorrhoea to penicillin in South-east Asia all point to the possibility of a global crisis of infectious diseases. As with the environment, the dangers of a return to the era before antibiotics arise directly from the abuse of science and economic growth – in this case the excessive prescription of antibiotics in developed countries and their inclusion in animal feed.

Here we see in its most dramatic form an instance of the double challenge of globalization – the worldwide incidence of disease, and the grotesque inequalities both in the incidence of such diseases and the medical resources to deal with them. These processes are not taking place in nature, but within social and political systems that shape, and accentuate, their consequences. Provision of medical care in all forms is one of the most striking of all indexes of global inequality: those affected by HIV in the west can have its affects mitigated by a cocktail of anti-retroviral drugs. But that cocktail costs over $10,000 a year, something the many millions of sufferers in Africa cannot afford.[9] The same applies to the impact of future scientific and technological change. If through the revolution in the life sciences genetic make-up can be adjusted, and lifespan greatly enhanced, then social and political relations will be affected too. As with all new discoveries, those with money will have access to these, whereas those without will not: the prospect of a world divided by wealth but also by access to genetic treatment is, at best, profoundly unsettling.

The same concern for the differential distribution of technology applies to information technology: much is made of the egalitarian, emancipatory potential of the IT revolution. Anyone can publish, communicate, trade. But there is a darker side to all this. First there is what has come to be termed the 'digital divide', inequality of access to the very equipment and networks needed. Those who do gain access may easily find themselves relegated to the margins by rapid changes in both hardware and software. Second, IT networks allow new, and potentially, sinister forms of control, by governments and those with monopoly power over the software and licences. Mergers in the USA between news broadcasters, Internet companies and the entertainment industry do not bode well for freedom of expression in the media, or for independent, plural voices. Third, the possibility of any critical or independent voice, in politics or anywhere else, depends on the ability to distinguish between the reliability and quality of different material. The information super-highway is also an information super-junkyard. Where everything is jumbled up, such discrimination, the necessary prerequisite for political and social responsibility, becomes more difficult.

The world is not, and never was, short of information. What it is short of is the ability of people, educated to think, and if necessary to take their time before they pronounce judgement, in a critical and original way. It is far from evident that the IT explosion enhances this process. What is more, its social and cultural consequences – the challenge to established forms of social life, be they in education, child-rearing or personal relationships – cannot yet be gauged. Intimacy and reflection may be casualties. The inability of people to switch off is a recipe for global neurosis. It may be that IT will, like earlier forms of dramatic changes in communication, the telephone or the television, be absorbed by established forms of learning and social interaction: the consequences may, however, be far greater.

What is most striking, and disturbing, about the current prevailing climate of scientific optimism, or indeed the environmental pessimism that is its mirror image, is a shared fatalism, the way they downplay the emphasis on human agency. The information or biological 'revolutions' are talked about as if they are nothing to do with people, but are simply products of inevitable or structural change. The same used to be said of the arms race – weapons became 'outdated', they had to be 'modernized', as if somehow they had an organic life of their own. But it is precisely in

such areas that human agency is most needed: not as a fatalistic
adjustment to some inexorable process that is somehow taking place
'out there', but taking control of and responsibility for that process,
defending what is threatened, and making the best use of what
science now offers. This applies above all to new developments in
the life sciences. Fatalism of another kind besets so much discussion
of the environment, reflecting a lack of political will and a time-
scale of politicians that is ill-adjusted to meeting the onset of longer-
term environmental challenges.

The Unanswered Challenge: Modernity and Inequality

In the framework of arguably half a millennium of globalization, we
have in modern times already seen two ambitious, but crude,
attempts to address the problem of the gap between the developed
and less developed worlds: from 1870 to 1945 we had colonialism,
from 1945 to 1990 we had the experiment by around 20 countries
with communism. Both were, in their authoritarian, modernist
manner, developmentalist projects: they sought to transform relations between rich and poor countries. Both have now, after enormous cost, been discarded. The question remains as to whether a
third attempt to create a unified world, by way of globalization, can
do any better, and at less human cost.

The challenges raised by the global distribution of wealth and
science are, next to war, the most enduring and morally compelling
on the international agenda. Modernity, for all the economic and
political dynamism it has generated in some countries, has not
solved this question: indeed it was the expansion of the European
economic and political system across the world which created the
unequal, but united, world of today. In the form in which it has
spread in the 1980s and 90s, this economic system, now subsumed
in the term 'globalization', has in many ways made inequalities of
distribution worse.

The responsibility for overcoming the inequality inherent in globalization lies, in the first place, with the state. The market alone can
solve neither the instabilities, now accelerated by rapid communications, nor the inequalities, and resentments, that it generates. This
above all is the lesson of critical reflection on the twentieth
century.[10] Because the market alone cannot resolve these issues,

there should not be excessive expectations about what can be achieved by multinational corporations: they are only in part the source, or the solution, of the problems of the world's economic system. It remains essentially the function of states to maintain the stability of the system and to ensure that policies designed significantly to reduce inequality, in economic, technological and social terms, are introduced. An example of this can be found in the development of a 'global financial architecture', designed to offset crises in the international markets. Although this is often discussed as if it was about some vague interlocking of independent financial bodies, it is first and foremost a matter of how *states* can collaborate, through early warning systems and codes of good practice, and co-ordinate emergency bail-outs.

Furthermore, an architecture is only as strong as the bricks that comprise it: the basis for state interaction is that these states themselves are effective and honest – the internal dimension of global governance (see Chapter 9). The result can be that their joint actions can forestall and offset the dangers posed by globalization. In many ways, globalization makes the state more, not less, necessary. If agency is not found here, it is found nowhere. This relates, however, not only to the states of the more powerful countries – the Group of 8 (G8) and the OECD – but also to the states in developing societies. Economic changes on their own will not overcome the gap between richer and poorer states: this requires effective, well-run states to administer economic change. Here contemporary globalization reproduces its own inequalities: it sustains not only systems of globalized economic inequality, but the creation within poorer societies of weak, corrupt states that reinforce the inequality by recycling money back to the richer ones and are incapable of developing their own economies.

The state may also play a role in addressing another aspect of globalization, that of the increasing similarity of states, economies and societies, even cultures. In certain direct ways globalization does entail this: common rules for trade, investment, copyright, a shared set of legal and political principles around good governance and democracy. In the cultural sphere, be it elite or mass, other common trends are evident. A broad *homogenization* of societies is part of this process. Some homogenization may be a product not of globalization as such, that is, of external influences on any specific society, but more of the very common requirements of modern life: that every country has to have traffic laws is not a result of globalization so much as of the dictates of industrial society. How far globalization pushes towards a broad social and political homogeneity is less clear: countries can have different electoral, or jury, systems, speak different languages, prepare different food. It is taste, not global forces, that produces a shared youth culture.

In the realm of culture, the state, however, retains important margins of influence, both through the education system, which is not determined by globalization, and through the power to promote culture in all its dimensions. Here is another domain where the market alone cannot deliver: the catastrophic evolution of the world cinema industry, dominated by the products of Hollywood, is evidence enough of that – not that Hollywood does not produce many good films, but that its monopoly destroys cultural diversity. The cultural desert of TV film channels in the English-speaking world is index enough of this. A globalization that led to cultural uniformity would be a disaster for humanity: it is neither a desirable, nor a necessary, consequence of changes in the organisation of the world economy.

In a very broad sense, globalization represents the last, best chance for the system that drives it, capitalism. This is not a challenge which the rich and powerful can simply ignore. The twentieth century ended with a worldwide denunciation of the inequalities associated with globalization, from the protests at one-sided trade liberalization at the Seattle conference and the *Jubilee 2000* campaign for the reduction in the debt of poorer states to a diffuse challenging of the power of multinational corporations in developed and developing societies.

Ultimately, this is a question about the potential of capitalism itself. Those who endorse it, as in the neo-liberal arguments of today, believe it has limitless potential for growth *and* for the distribution of good: the market, we are told, *can* solve the problems it confronts. It is capable of constant innovation. The failure of capitalism to do this so far is, it is argued, a result either of lack of time, or of the obstacles – political, cultural, legal – which are placed in the way of its expansion. The counter-argument is that capitalism not only destroys much of what it transforms, *necessarily* producing an unequal world, divided along oligarchic lines, but that it too has its limits: in the nineteenth century they were those of the market itself, in the twenty-first they are, among other things, those of nature.

There remains some room for an open verdict. Capitalism has, in the past, been charged with being 'incapable' of providing a number of things which it later turned out to be able to yield: universal suffrage, legal equality of men and women, decolonization, industrialization in the Third World, the end of war between developed states. It has, on the other hand, had many chances and made many fine promises, which it has not fulfilled. It remains an open question whether, five centuries on from its initial expansion, this system can achieve the potential which its advocates ascribe to it, and diffuse its opportunities across the world: until, and unless, it does, then globalization will be but another word for the hegemony of a minority of rich states over the rest. This time round, capitalism has no excuses.

6

The Fragility of Democracy

Alongside war and inequality, the third of the great challenges facing the world at 2000 is that of extending, but also consolidating, democracy. Democratic states not only fulfil desirable political goals, and protect rights, they may also bring wealth and security. Fukuyama and others have claimed that democracy is the highest, implicitly final, stage of political development, and the one that is most compatible with other goals, notably economic growth. The fate of democracy is also of great import for any survey of international relations because of its close relation to peace. The intuition of Immanuel Kant at the end of the eighteenth century, that a peaceful international order could be founded through the co-operation of constitutional states, has now become a more proximate possibility.[1]

Those who argue that we live today in a democratic age point to the wave of democratizations in the 1990s in the former communist countries and in some parts of the Third World.[2] These have built upon the democratic legacy of the the struggles of the 'Short Twentieth Century', between and within states discussed in Chapter 2. A number of factors contributed to this development, of which the ideological exhaustion of alternative, anti-democratic trends is one, the association of democracy with economic prosperity is a second, and the reinforcement by the international community of democratic norms is a third. The number of countries certified as 'democratic' by basic electoral and constitutional criteria is rising by the year: from around 56 in 1990 to 86 in 2000. This trend is often used to reinforce a more general claim about the contemporary world: in the aftermath of the cold war, it is argued, the argument for liberal democracy has been won, there are no global contenders. With all sorts of hiccups, democratization is spreading across the world.

Liberty and its Limits

The claim promoted by much discussion of democracy is that it is, in some ways, an attainable goal, a political and constitutional order which, once achieved, is permanent. This is, of course, a modernist illusion, since democracy is a system which, as much as any other, can itself change or die. While most attention has been paid to the spread of democracy to hitherto undemocratic societies, of equal importance has been the re-evaluation of democratic politics within apparently established democratic states. Here there has been a widespread attempt not just to preserve but to rethink and creatively develop the forms of democratic political system that exist. A central assumption of many political orders, the finality of their constitutional development, has been challenged, reminding us that political forms are never static and wither if they do not develop. One example of such rethinking has been that of constitutional reform within hitherto apparently settled states – the recognition of diversity of region and culture in states such as Britain, Italy and France, the exploration of new forms of cultural and minority rights within historically colonial states such as Australia and Canada. All of this has been accompanied by a re-examination of the very histories of states, ethnicity and culture, and ultimately of power within these countries, a process encouraged by the dual acknowledgement of contemporary diversity, brought about by immigration, and historic diversity, long denied by narratives of national unity and hegemony.

Changes within modern society and the end of the cold war divide have also promoted thinking about the enhancement of democracy in developed societies, this often accompanied by attempts to reduce barriers between political traditions that the past century or two had divided – socialism and liberalism, reform and revolution, planning and market. In this perspective, 1989 marked the end, not of one, but of two ideologies – central planning and state direction on the one side, the free market dogmas of neo-liberalism on the other.[3] Instead a form of compromise, sometimes formulated in the form of a new centrist consensus, advocating a 'social market', was articulated. This stressed the restructuring of the state, taking it away from traditional forms of direction but giving it new functions within society, the development of a broad civic culture on such issues as education, the family and crime, a rethinking of full employment to link it much more closely to education and continuous re-education, the reconstruction of the welfare system, and an active engagement with the global dimension. Rather timidly proclaimed in the English-speaking world, where the force of neo-liberalism remains strong, above all under the shadow of the USA, but more vigorously espoused by social-democratic thinkers in France, Germany and the Scandinavian countries, this approach reflects the double ideological crisis of the 1990s and the opportunities this has opened up.

While such reassessments may enhance democracy, it is in this conditional and changing character of democracy that the greatest of contemporary illusions may lie. For any democratic order is vulnerable to important counter-arguments which not only continue to apply, but which have in some respects been accentuated by recent socio-economic changes within modern society and by international changes associated with globalization. Democratic orders in the major OECD states are *not* in imminent danger of collapse, as they were in much of Europe in the late 1920s and 30s: they are, however, subject to a range of critiques that post-1989 triumphalism may have understated.

These critiques fall into three categories: theoretical, conjunctural, global. The theoretical critique of democracy, as long-standing as democracy itself, challenges the appearance of *formal* equality in the public realm. A focus on political, or electoral and legal forms alone, conceals the persistence of other, inherently undemocratic, features of modern society and political life. In ancient Greece the critique focused on *ochlocracy* (that is, rule by the mob), that the mass of voters were ill-equipped, by formation and temperament, to exercise a responsible vote. Conservative thinkers in the twentieth century took fright at the entry of the masses into politics, without justification. On the other hand, the dangers of the tyranny of the majority, always present, take a particularly virulent form in societies of ethnic and communal diversity and where minority rights are not adequately protected. An equally powerful critique of democracy, and indeed of liberalism as a whole, begins, and ends, with the conflict between the appearance of equality and neutrality of political form, and the reality of inequality and partisanship produced by money: the conflict between democracy and market relations is evident in the ability of business-friendly politicians to influence outcomes by the amount of campaign expenditure at their disposal, in the role of the press in distorting information and elec-

toral choice, and, even were the electoral process itself to be free of
distortions by the market, in the ability of those with financial power
to circumvent government entirely.

Both these critiques have, in considerable measure, been accentuated by trends in contemporary society. Modern equivalents of
ochlocracy, on issues such as capital punishment, immigration and
gender rights, let alone the responsibilities of international politics,
are not hard to find. Across the world nationalism and chauvinism
have, for their part, abused majority rule: the fate of Catholics in
Northern Ireland between the 1920s and 1970s, or of Muslims in
India, says little for the wisdom of the majority. The abuses of
democracy are in considerable measure accentuated by the demagogy of politicians. As for the distortions of elections by money,
these are commonplace in every developed society. Elections apart,
government too is restricted, shaped, thwarted by financial and business interest. The most consistently irresponsible part of the political process is that which is, historically, seen as the embodiment of
civil society, namely the press. As we shall see in Chapter 9, this is
undermining not just democracy within states but also governance at
the global level. Throughout the developed world, and particularly
in the USA and the UK, the independence of the press of corporate
interest, and their ability to establish an independent stance on
matters requiring political judgement, has declined.

The classical theoretical critique of democracy has, however, been
reinforced in ways that compound scepticism about the finality of
any political order. First of all, feminism has, in both its first, early
twentieth-century form and in its second wave, from the 1960s
onwards, articulated a devastating critique of established political
forms, both in the manner in which equality for women in the public
sphere – economic, legal, social, educational as well as political – is
denied, and in the ways in which a mere public equality, in, say,
voting or eligibility of office, leaves unaddressed the inequalities
that persist in the domestic, ideological and social spheres. Like the
socialist critique of liberalism, the feminist critique undermines the
formal criteria of democracy itself. Second, the environmental
movement has, in ways that are only beginning to be clear, questioned the ability of modern society to sustain its prosperity and lifestyle without profound economic changes *and* infringements of what
has hitherto been seen as the realm of personal liberty. The ecological critique not only challenges the power of corporations to

consume and pollute, but the very autonomy of the consumer, as manifest in market and election alike. Above all, it brings us back to one of the most long-established critiques of the democratic process, its limitation to the time-scale of electoral renewal: processes that accumulate over decades, or centuries, are not addressed by elections, and political horizons, of three to five years.

To these two, more contemporary, forms of theoretical critique there has, in recent years, been added a third, philosophical critique which, often in the guise of liberalism itself, seeks not to enhance but to curtail the potential of democracy by questioning its universality. The conservative argument that only some peoples are capable of democracy, or that if others are it may take them centuries to get there, has long been familiar: it was, after all, a stock in trade of colonialism. It has, however, been revived in two other, apparently divergent, forms. One is the argument, espoused by rulers and their defenders, with regard to non-European regions of the world, notably the Arab world and East Asia, to the effect that 'western' democracy is inappropriate for these societies, conflicting as it does with indigenous values. The other is the argument advocated by some liberal philosophers, according to which non-western societies should be allowed to maintain non-democratic forms of government, provided they respect basic rules of order.[4] These questionings of democracy involve a double challenge, a set of sociological arguments affirming the essential difference of cultures *and* the legitimacy of interpretations thereof by elites and authorities of them, and a philosophical challenge to the principle of universality. The former will be examined in Chapter 8, the latter in Chapter 10. Suffice it to say here that the claim of difference, like that of 'authenticity', may conceal more than it reveals.

These theoretical challenges to democracy, from those who wish to strengthen it as from those who limit its application, have in considerable measure been reinforced by modern society, both within developed societies, where democratic forms prevail, and in the context of the international spread of democracy. The contemporary world provides, therefore, a second major, conjunctural, set of reasons for being concerned about the consolidation of democracy: this is, above all, because of the spread, in a situation marked precisely by the collapse of old ideologies and forms of civic responsibility on the one hand and, on the other, by the diffusion by globalization, of ideological forms that threaten values of tolerance within and between societies.

While OECD democracy is not under imminent threat of constitutional collapse, there is throughout the developed world a widespread erosion of confidence in democracy. This involves disillusion with the intentions and capacities of politicians, distrust of the public sector and a decline in any belief in public service. While constitutional change or reform is under discussion in many countries, certain long-established forms of democracy have fallen into disarray: in many developed countries local, city, government has become a byword for corruption and ineffectiveness, and attracts decreasing political interest; the notion of democracy at the place of work, through forms of council or consultation, has become less and less an object of public discussion, let alone practice. In the case of the latter, of course, globalization provides a ready excuse for dispensing with what is now branded as an 'outmoded' practice.

At the same time there is a growing resort in many countries, especially those emerging from communist rule, to nationalism.[5] Nationalism is not inherently incompatible with democracy, although it often is, precisely because it invests legitimacy in an atavistic concept, the historically given nation, and in those, the 'leaders' of some kind or another, who claim to represent this legitimacy. The coincidence of strong nationalism with anti-democratic politics is too strong to dismiss as casual. Yet whatever its variations may be with regard to domestic politics, nationalism most certainly is invariant as regards relations with other states and peoples: here competition, the exaggeration of differences and the denial of co-operative solutions become the norm. In its milder forms this may take the rejection of international agreements on trade or the environment, a chauvinist stance on immigration, and a self-righteousness rejection of criticisms of a country's human rights policies – witness not only the vociferous and transparent response of countries such as China, Iran or Israel to exposure of their use of torture, but the US reaction to criticisms by Amnesty International of its penal system and use of capital punishment, and British indignation at decisions of the European Court of Human Rights. In its more extreme form, as in former Yugoslavia, the surge of nationalism associated with the 1990s has led to murder and humanitarian crime on a large scale.

To these theoretical and conjunctural challenges associated with the functioning of democracy *within* societies, and the tensions of contemporary politics, may be added the challenges of globalization itself. Here a contradictory process is certainly at work. In some ways the democratization of the last quarter of the twentieth century has itself been encouraged by international processes. In the 1970s, European countries that had been under fascist rule turned to democracy in order the better to participate in the prosperity and status of the European Common Market. The Portuguese revolution of 1974 had a militant, revolutionary socialist component: but the main force behind it, and the main beneficiary, was a middle class intent on ending Portugal's isolation from the rest of Europe, and its links to a burdensome pre-modern empire in Africa, and becoming a 'normal' part of Europe. Similarly, in the 1990s, countries in Latin America and in eastern Europe were drawn, and in some cases pulled, towards greater respect for democratic norms: the Council of Europe, for example, has imposed conditions with regard to elections, minority and gender rights on countries wishing to join it and, by extension, the EU itself. It is not a denial of these influences to point out that the encouragement of democracy by the major western states was itself highly partial and conditional. In the cold war, strategic interest led to the indulgence, when not creation, of authoritarian regimes; in the post-cold-war epoch, the encouragement of democracy stopped short where, as was most spectacularly the case with allies in the Arab world, a continued conflict between strategic and economic interest and democratization prevailed.

Yet globalization promotes other anti-democratic influences that both compound those trends associated with earlier critiques, and create new difficulties for democratic rule. In the first place, globalization, by restricting the ability of states to manage their economies and finances, allows for much greater variations in living standards than was previously the case. Such fluctuations, and the opening up of frontiers, open up more room for mass movements of protest to mobilize on nationalist grounds. In both hegemonic and hegemonized societies, the temptations of nationalist demagogy, and a rejection of international co-operation, have increased. On the Japanese, British and US right, for example, this tone is recurrent. For decades past we have seen the use of resistance to external, social and intellectual influences by authoritarian states and movements disguised as resistance to 'cultural imperialism': globalization threatens to accentuate this, as those who wish to manipulate their own peoples resort more and more to denunciations of external influences.

A similar ambivalent impact may be associated with the spread of the Internet and e-commerce. These, on the one hand, 'empower' those in search of goods and information. Yet they also create a world in which traditional, democratic controls on the diffusion of prejudicial and mendacious materials are eroded, and in which the collection of taxes, the financial bases of states, is more difficult, even as forms of intrusion in the private sphere, by corporate and state bodies, increases. Some have suggested that democracy can be enhanced by what is termed e-government: but this, with its promise of instant access and consultation, will erode the influence of those without such access or the time to participate in such activities. An ever-active e-democracy, backed by the disproportionate intervention of special interests and by a sensational and irresponsible media, would be fraud indeed, an ochlocratic nightmare.

Historical Context

The challenges to democracy as a political form – theoretical, conjunctural and global – do not, however, mean that the liberal argument on democracy is invalid: rather these challenges are arguments for the defence of democracy, not for its abandonment. Democracy is in some form or another the most desirable political form. It has shown itself to be compatible with economic liberalism and growth. There are indeed no global ideological rivals at the moment – on this the much abused Francis Fukuyama is broadly right. Nationalism is not a rival ideology, since it does not prescribe for internal political orders, and religious fundamentalism is neither global nor, in any economic sense, an answer: on closer examination it too lacks a coherent model of political order. The argument on democracy and peace also has much validity: both on a priori grounds, because of the reluctance of constitutional states to go to war, and on the historical record that to date no properly democratic states have fought, it is a sustainable hypothesis that democracies do not go to war with each other. This is of great significance for the future: a world in which there was broadly distributed prosperity *and* established liberal democracy, a global EU if you like, would be one in which the spectre of war would be remote. The point is, of course, that we are a long way from it. The zone of peace formed by developed states is threatened, from without *and* from within.

Here it is worth putting the consolidation of democracy in historical context. Democracy can be defined as a constitutional or republican order, in which one person one vote operates, and in which there is reasonable rotation of office-holders. There must also be a time test as well: democracy can only be said to be consolidated when it has been there for a period of time – a generation, twenty-five years or so, at least. We have seen too many ephemeral 'democracies' – the Weimar Republic in the 1920s, Lebanon, Sri Lanka, many Latin American and African states in the 1960s and 70s. With this definition and time test, democracy is a very recent acquisition, even in the most developed countries: women did not get the vote in France until 1948, millions of blacks were only enfranchised in the USA in the 1960s, in one part of the United Kingdom, that is, Northern Ireland, the electoral system was characterized by serious irregularities until the 1970s.[6]

At the same time, it would, as already suggested, be complacent to assume that this system is, once established, bound to continue: there is no finality in human affairs. Political systems, like buildings, need maintenance: if they do not get it, they start to crumble, and fall down (leaving aside what the more unruly occupants themselves may do). No one looking at the state of democracies in the developed world today can fail to be uneasy: falling levels of electoral participation in the USA; almost universal concern with the distortion of electoral process by private funding, lobbyists and special interests; a declining level of political literacy on many fronts, especially the international; widespread disregard by younger people for politicians and participation in political life; a rather dramatic paucity of credible political leaders. The fall in public trust in political institutions affects most developed countries. If these trends are extrapolated over coming decades, the edifice could be very shaky indeed by 2050.[7] We cannot and should not therefore assume that democracy will continue to last for ever in the absence of renewal and reform. At the same time, there are worrying ideological trends on the horizon: in the USA the religious right, an estimated 80 million, exerts a serious negative influence on political and social life. In Europe the rise of a new far-right in the Alpine world – Austria and Switzerland – may be a singular and short-lived process: it may, on the other hand, be the first sign of a very nasty trend indeed, which will find echo in other, more powerful, states. The potential of capitalism to generate extremism of the left may be in abeyance. That to generate extremism of the right may not.

If we turn to the rest of the world, the picture is also none too rosy. Of the 195 states in the world, up to 100 may be classed as 'democratic' on some formal criteria. The number who pass the time test, and who have real alternation of office-holders, is much smaller: OECD states, India, parts of the Caribbean, perhaps 40 states in all. Many others are, or may be, in transition to democracy, but they are just as often in transition to nothing: they are what they are, semi-democratic, semi-authoritarian states where an appearance of electoral power is accompanied by either formal, or informal, control by dictators or oligarchies. Every dictatorship in the world has learned to play the certification and compliance game. I once asked someone in a semi-authoritarian state that allowed a multiplicity of parties and some diversity in the press 'Why do you have pluralism in your country?' 'Because the president told us to have pluralism' came the answer.

In addition to claims about formal electoral politics, we hear much about the need for civil society and NGOs, and rightly so. But, as discussed in Chapter 3, many NGOs are fronts, run by the states – what Amnesty calls 'GINGOs', government-run NGOs – while others are subjected to extensive forms of political, legal and financial control. Even in those areas where democratization appears to have swept all before it, everything is not quite as it appears: the success of Hugo Chávez in Venezuela in 1998 was a triumph *against* electoral politics. By contrast, the Pakistani generals won widespread support in 1999 when they ousted corrupt elected civilians.

Russia, China, Indonesia

This uneven and conditional spread of democracy is pertinent, in the context of the argument of this book, above all to the question of peace. If so many countries in the world are not democratic, and may well not become so in the near future, then the risks of war remain high. It has, indeed, been convincingly argued that the most dangerous states are not dictatorships at all, but states in the process of democratization – passions run high, leaders lack control, social and economic tensions may be extreme.[8] The great conflicts of the twentieth century were generated in contexts of rapid political and social change. In this regard there are three countries whose internal political development should give particular concern.

As already noted, Russia has far from resolved the problems which have followed from the collapse of the USSR. In the 15 former Soviet states, where GDP in 1998 was on average 50% that of 1989, democracy in the proper sense exists only in the three Baltic countries; Russia is at best semi-democratic, marked by lawlessness and media controls and now dominated by an authoritarian faction issued from part of the former KGB; all the others, without exception, are forms of political dictatorship. Even those, such as Armenia, which exhibited some democratic culture in the immediate aftermath of the fall of communism, have now made another transition, to dictatorship, kleptocracy or rule by thieves, and, where necessary, violence against political opponents. Political legitimacy is therefore weak, politics and administration are riven with corruption, violence is endemic in commercial and political life.

As in all former Soviet countries, there has been a massive fall in living standards in the Russian Federation. There is nostalgia for past security, and considerable longing, as Vladimir Putin, elected President in March 2000, knows well, for a strong leader. The most immediate dangers to international security lie in the inadequate controls over Russian nuclear and other military equipment. The longer-run danger is of a Russia that remains in political and economic turmoil, and where political leadership resorts more and more to demagogy at home, and abroad. The war in the north Caucasian republic of Chechnya may, arguably, be a one-off, a product of the particular history and political character of that region: but throughout the Russian Federation there are broader, irresolvable and explosive, tensions.

China is apparently in a better situation: its economy boomed in the 1990s, its leadership remains in political and military control. A definite liberalization of political life is taking place. The great unanswered question is whether China can continue on this road of economic change without political change, and without social upheaval. The system of control by the party is eroding, without any other system replacing it. This political transition is all the more difficult because of the social tensions which economic change is producing: rising corruption and criminality, great inequalities between coastal and interior regions, mass lay-offs from state firms. Social pressures may rise as China's population is expected to reach 1.5 billion by 2050. One index of the crisis of political authority in China has been the recurrence, to no visible effect, of campaigns against corruption. In May 2000 the Communist Party published 'A Great Programme for Comprehensively Strengthening Party Building', a 74-page directive designed to revitalize the party. The campaign was, as ever with Chinese communist edicts, phrased in numerical terms, this time as the 'Three Represents': the party must represent the most advanced part of China's economy, culture and the fundamental interests of the people.[9] Few believe that China can sustain this resistance to political change for long; even fewer can see how and when the necessary change can be achieved.

The dangers of the Indonesian situation have been vividly evident since 1998. The violence unleashed in 1999, with state approval, against the population of East Timor, once it had voted in a UN referendum for independence, was one index of this. The growing inter-communal violence in outlying islands and a mass of unresolved issues of secession are matched by weakness of governmental authority at the centre. In the wings lie those who have wrought such havoc on Indonesia in the past – potential military dictators on the one hand, and religious fundamentalists on the other. Indonesia, with a population of 204 million in 2000, is the world's fourth largest country, and the largest Islamic state. Its strategic position on the world's shipping lanes, its place in the financial and commercial system of East Asia and the already evident threat of its environmental degradation all make what happens there of acute concern to the whole world.

The Chimera of Fortress Democracy

The evolution of the modern world and, in particular, the changes of recent years have placed in question what had hitherto been a conventional assumption of much thinking about democracy, namely that the preconditions for it, and its orderly functioning, were largely if not wholly dependent on internal development. Democratic theory, conventionally understood, focused almost exclusively on the functioning of institutions *within* states, on relations between government and people, and appropriate mechanisms for dealing with them. The international dimensions were regarded, where not ignored entirely, as something additional, 'out there'. In three senses at least this was never a sustainable assumption. First of all, the whole history of political development within countries has been closely associated with their relations with other states – above all through the state being compelled to make concessions to its citizens by its need to mobilize them for war. Second, those political theorists who, at first reading, seemed concerned exclusively with the internal preconditions for democracy – be it Locke, Rousseau, Burke or Mill – made important assumptions about the external: not least about the relation of their own political institutions to those of others and the need for a broad similarity between them. Political theorists were in this sense not explicitly, but implicitly, international in perspective. Third, the history of the rise of democracy *within* the developed world was accompanied by a very contrasted history *without*, the export of illiberalism to the less advanced part of the world, be this through colonial rule and its coercive maintenance on the one hand, or the sustaining, in the cold war, of authoritarian regimes on the other. The classical theory and history of democracy have, therefore, an inherently international dimension.

The contemporary world reinforces this dependence. Democracy presupposes a global order within which it can function. This is the Achilles heel of the widespread belief in the possibilities of insulating the developed, and democratic, world from the rest, of a gated community of democratic states functioning without challenge from the world beyond the walls. The British diplomat Robert Cooper has famously suggested a three-part typology of states in the world – the pre-modern or failed states, the modern or strong authoritarian states, and the post-modern, which, as in Europe, pool sovereignty and no longer operate according to classical conventions of security and balance of power.[10] The problem is, as he himself discusses, how far the conceptual distinctions made can be sustained in the real world, for the security and prosperity, and good conscience, of the post-modern are under challenge from the pre-modern and the modern. To the long-established linkages between democratic order within and the international system without are now added the pressures which globalization itself has promoted.

The external pressures on democracy may be summarized under five headings. First, the world economy: a world economy means to a considerable degree global vulnerability. If the world economy was not compartmentalized into secure units immune to each other's fluctuations in 1929, it is even less so now. Events 'outside the wire' may have an important influence on the prosperity of developed countries: commodity prices and financial fluctuations in unstable markets to name but two. The reduction in global reserves of oil will, sooner or later, pose a dramatic challenge to the technology and very way of life of consumers in developed countries. Second, environment and health: the steady rise in the pollution of the atmosphere and oceans, the global spread of killer diseases, old and new, the depletion of resources, the very melting of icecaps as a result of ecological change will, if not dramatically, then over time come to affect every society on the earth. Third, migration: the pressures for movement from poor to richer countries continue to increase, even as the obstacles to economic migration in most developed countries remain as high as ever. This will lead both to a growth in illegal migration, and to a growing resentment within the south at the failure to permit such movement, hence the need for an explicit, global regime on movement of peoples. Fourth, security: the fears of American nuclear planners about attacks by Third World states may be mistaken, but other forms of challenge, to individuals travelling in poorer states and through forms of low-level attack on the citizens and territories of developed states, may increase.

Finally, there is responsibility: states are bound, not least by signature to the UN Charter, to work collectively to uphold international peace and security; many individuals, and intermittently the media, in developed states are concerned to respond to human or political disasters elsewhere. Much as the realists of the right, and the more unreconstructed anti-imperialists of the left, may wish this concern would go away, it will not, spasmodically as it may be expressed. The claim made that there is an 'international community' or 'international society', a set of states with shared values, too easily avoids the fact that this was created by force, and that great inequalities of wealth and power subsist between states. The argument that there *are* some shared values, however – and that the claims of those without wealth and power are about getting more of them, and seeing standards more consistently applied – is far more sustainable.

The fate of democracy is therefore, as it always was, international. The emphasis of much contemporary debate is on how democracy itself may spread, to encompass other areas of the world – the modern and the pre-modern in Robert Cooper's terms, the 'realignment of the provinces' in the language of Hegel and Fukuyama. That there are important, at least contemporary, forces working in this direction is self-evident: but the recent wave of democratization may falter, just as states learn to adjust and disguise their retention of authoritarian power. Within the European continent, there are powerful instruments for the encouragement of democracy, as there are, to a lesser extent, in Latin America and India. Elsewhere, however, the balance of political and social forces is less favourable to a sustained democratization. Yet this concern with the international spread of democratization to the non-democratic world is given greater, not less, urgency by the converse process, the impact on the democratic world of other states and societies. The temporary opportunity provided for the development of democracy in the late twentieth and early twenty-first century may be sustained. It may, on the other hand, be eroded, by a decline in democratic commitment within and a resilience of authoritarian states and ruling elites without.

7

The Unaccountable Hegemon

In any survey of the world at 2000, the question of the USA, of how to analyse it, and how to evaluate what it does, and does not do, is central. Not only is the USA the dominant power in the world, and likely to remain so for the foreseeable future, but the changes taking place within it, and which shape to a considerable degree the lives of those who live in the rest of the world, are a challenge to any social scientist or thinking person. In the mid-nineteenth century Marx analysed British industrial society because, he believed, it set the pattern for the rest of the world. The same argument, a century and a half later, applies to the USA: it is the *hegemon*, an informal ruler that is at once dominant power and dominant model. Marx was wrong about the world imitating Britain, but right to see it as an engine of change worldwide.

America is the object of more controversy and denunciation than any other power, and this too merits recognition and discussion. Pious loyalty to Washington, or frenzied praise for Silicon Valley, is without foundation. Yet unreflective anti-American sentiment is a widespread, rather easy, option for left and right around the world, and may conceal more than it reveals. In the last months of his life, French President François Mitterand was to remark:

> France does not realize it, but we are at war with America. Yes, permanent war, vital – an economic war... They are hard, those Americans. They are voracious. They want undivided power over the world.[1]

Views about America, for or against, also underlie much discussion of many international questions, be they the crises of the late 1990s –

Kosovo, Bosnia, Kuwait, East Timor – or the management of the world economy, the WTO, GM foods. Arguments about both the future of modern society and international politics are therefore, to a considerable degree, an argument about America.

Any assessment of the USA today, and of its possible futures, must encompass, first of all, analysis of the country itself, its history, culture and domestic politics, something that is remarkably weak in academic, press and public contexts outside America. What passes for understanding of the USA is too often automatic, either adulation and mimesis or its opposites, denunciation, conspiracy theory or cultural conservatism. There is a need, growing with each decade, to discriminate in regard to the lifestyle and culture of America, to separate out that which is desirable from that which is not, and to recognize different strands in American culture itself. There is, in sum, a need to distinguish between the automatic denunciation of the USA found in large parts of the left and right internationally and a measured, informed engagement with what the USA has done and could do, as well as with the very varied and ongoing debate within the USA itself.

This need to discriminate pertains as much as anything to the twin engines of contemporary, if impermanent, success: the market and information technology. For some, these have provided the answer to the problems of modern economic and social change, for others, they reproduce and intensify inequality and a neglect of public goods, and public responsibilities, which are at the heart of a stable, just society. The strengths of US society are evident, and never more so than now: this is a society with unparalleled economic success, and scientific and technological achievement; which has, with the exception of black Americans, pioneered multi-racialism, and whose federal political system is of proven adaptability. But there is much too that could threaten it, from within and without. From within we see a range of social problems, a degraded popular culture, falling electoral participation. In the euphoria of the IT boom it is worth recalling earlier crashes, and the frail, bubble-like elements of the e-commerce boom. For all the talk of a 'new economy', computers, software and telecommunications accounted in 2000 for less than 10% of GDP. In the central element of political life, leadership, and its moral and intellectual requirements, America has, as it were, been underachieving.

Internationally, there are, in the time-frame of a decade or two, no major rivals, and few threats. But US domination and the reflexes and tone of unilateralism are promoting a global resentment that is as unhealthy for those who fall prey to it as it is ominous for the USA itself. In the economic field, we cannot know whether the current US boom will continue, or for how long, nor can we see the longer-run social and intellectual consequences of the continuing IT revolution: this is sometimes spoken of as a new frontier, yet it is a frontier that is itself limitless. Contemporary American capitalism, however, generates not just new forms of organization and production, but also new ideals, new aspirations, and new forms of agency, individual and collective. Thomas Friedman has argued, in his praise for the American way of life, for a combination of selected tradition and desirable modernity, the olive tree and the Lexus car. He argues against an undifferentiated response, as to what to accept and reject, and indeed as to what it is that America, and other countries, offer. He is right that the argument should be about this balance, if not necessarily in his own answer as to what this balance should be. Modernity, like tradition, is plural and diverse in the twenty-first as much as in the nineteenth and twentieth centuries.

As the world enters the twenty-first century, no question is therefore of greater importance, or more likely to affect our lives, than the future of the USA, both as an international power and a social model. This is the country which, with a population of 275 million, 4% of the world total, has emerged from the end of the cold war and the onset of globalization as the dominant power – in strategic and military terms (the defence budget of $300 billion is equal to that of the next six countries combined), in terms of political and diplomatic influence, and in terms of the multiple appeals of its lifestyle. This is virtually the only developed country with a fast-growing population. By 2100 there will, it is estimated, be 571 million Americans. Be it in clothes, music, food, gender relations, the aspirations of a modern lifestyle, or IT, America is where the most influential changes are happening and to which the rest of the world must react. America also leads the world in scientific development, for better and for worse. At times, indeed, it is difficult to distinguish between globalization, in its many forms, and Americanization.

The appeal of America is felt across the world. This is in a nutshell the message of Friedman's *The Lexus and the Olive Tree*:

> We Americans are the apostles of the Fast World, the enemies of tradition, the prophets of the free market and the high priests of high tech. We want 'enlargement' of both our values and our Pizza

Huts. We want the world the follow our lead and become democratic, capitalistic, with a Web site in every pot, a Pepsi on every lip, Microsoft Windows in every computer and most of all – most of all – with everyone, everyone pumping their own gas.[2]

This is to a surprising degree reciprocated. Two centuries ago Goethe summed it up in his poem *Amerika, du hast es besser* – literally, 'America, you have it better'. It is worth speculating about what percentage of the world's population would like a Green Card allowing them to work legally in the USA. The answers may vary from a low of 40% to as high as 70%: much of Latin America and Africa, all or most of China and Russia, quite a lot of the Middle East. As Jean Baudrillard wrote:

> Whatever happens, and whatever one thinks of the arrogance of the dollar or the multinationals, it is this culture which, the world over, fascinates those very people who suffer most at its hands, and it does so through the deep, insane conviction that it has made all their dreams come true.[3]

This renewed attraction and power reflect both a reassertion of traditional forms of influence *and* new social and economic forms. Yet this domination of the USA is in many ways a surprising one. Only a decade or two ago there were those who stressed the decline of US power from its pre-eminent position, around 1950, when it accounted for 50% of world GNP. Other commercial powers – Europe, Japan – were on the rise. The Soviet military threat was still credible – all too credible, if right-wing US alarm about Soviet 'leads' in this or that branch of the arms race were to be taken seriously. Revolution – from Vietnam to Iran, from Angola to Nicaragua – was sweeping the Third World. While there were those, among them the British writers Susan Strange and Michael Cox, who disputed this, prevailing opinion went the other way.[4] Paul Kennedy was to publish in 1988 his influential *The Rise and Fall of the Great Powers*.[5] This suggested that the USA would, like its predecessors the Romans, the Dutch and the British, cease to be a world power as excess commitment, 'imperial overstretch', took its toll. US bookshops were full of tomes on the Japanese commercial challenge.

Then in 1989–91 came the end of communism. This may have looked like a clear US victory over the USSR, despite George

Bush's policy of 'no gloating'. But many was the American commentator who doubted this verdict. 'We all paid the price of the cold war', it was said. 'We're hurting too.'[6] The USA too had suffered through the arms race and the concentration of power in the national security state. Indeed, the liberal consensus seemed to be that the USA had not won the cold war at all. The crisis of the cities, racial tension, the overcrowded prisons, the very potholes on Fifth Avenue all showed how weak the USA really was. This retrospective argument about the costs to America of the cold war laid much emphasis on the political consequences of the conflict, the creation of a 'national security state'.

There are, however, reasons for doubting the conventional view of American crisis or decline even in the cold war period. On closer examination one may question the argument that the cold war weakened American democracy. The term 'national security state' implies that the US state could possibly not have had a national security component: what was unnatural was the belief, that existed until the 1940s, and which still survives in populist fears about foreigners in Washington (most recently Chinese political donors), that the 'republic' is necessarily corrupted by external engagements. Much is made, rightly, of McCarthyism, a cold war phenomenon that did reduce democracy in America by persecuting dissent: but against that regression in the early 1950s can be set the civil rights movement of the 1960s – a massive upsurge that led to the effective enfranchisement of millions of people. The civil rights movement had an international dimension: it was all the harder to resist precisely because of America's cold war pretension to lead the world in political values. The same scepticism applies to arguments about the corruption of the Washington political elite by contact with the outside world: the corruption, bombast, arrogance and mendacity of many US political leaders did not need the cold war. Dixie and Tammary Hall saw to that.

Most of the analysis of American weakness, military or economic, in the cold war was mistaken. The Soviets *never* led in the arms race, the brief period after the launch of *Sputnik 1* in 1957 being the one exception. Over the ensuing decade things began to look somewhat different. Militarily the USA remains even further ahead than ever of its rivals and allies: without the US role there would have been no international operations over Kuwait, Bosnia, Kosovo or even East Timor. The 'Revolution in Military Affairs' means that US initiatives in military procurement now include weaponry, such as a limited missile defence system, that no other country can match. While procurement budgets around the world were falling, US expenditure on purchases of military equipment was to go from $45 billion in 1997 to $68 billion in 2005, with the Pentagon arguing for a figure of $80 billion. In economic terms the USA has drawn decisively ahead of its commercial rivals in Europe and East Asia: sustained growth, technological acceleration, lower unemployment and low inflation gave the USA boom years under the Clinton administration. The budget deficit that seemed so intractable in the early 1990s disappeared. Internationally the dollar was supreme: in 1999, because so many people around the world were willing to hold dollars or invest in the USA, the USA could afford to run a trade deficit of $270 billion, on total imports of $1.23 trillion. Meanwhile Microsoft, America Online and myriad other clickers and servers created a new world, at once of profit, creativity and imagination, and potential social and intellectual destruction.

The world is flying blind when it comes to foreseeing the consequences of the technological change associated with the Internet revolution; whatever is in store, it will be America that will be the world's laboratory. In the world of the Internet, America has, uniquely, no need for a country code, an addressing suffix or top-level domain, at the end of the e-mail address: the rest of the world has, however, to identify itself to the global centre. The Internet itself was a by-product of US military research in the 1970s on secure communications, the Advanced Research Projects Agency. The very body that regulates cyberspace, ICANN, the Internet Corporation for Assigned Names and Numbers, is a non-profit corporation chartered by the US Commerce Department. In ways as yet only partially visible, American companies have already taken control of the infrastructure of the global communications network, in particular commercial websites and cyber-exchanges. Little wonder that a new mood of self-confidence and often arrogance has emerged in the USA. America is, it is said, the 'pre-eminent' power, the only superpower, the indispensable guarantor of world peace and prosperity. French critics refer to it as a *hyperpuissance*, a 'hyperpower'. Many were the prognostications made on the eve of the millennium that this would, even more than the last fifty years, be 'the American century'.

A Society in Change

Part of the political basis for this redefined international role is internal: not so much in terms of four-year electoral cycles but more in terms of the structural – that is, conjunctural – evolution of American society. The dominance of the old internationalist east coast establishment, which sustained engagement through World War II and the cold war, is over: it will not return. American society is itself adjusting to the rise of Latino and Asian immigration, and a consequent shift of influence, political and economic, from the east coast to the south and the west. Europe and the political commitments associated with the European engagement are receding. It is not possible to establish any direct, one-to-one relationship between the changing ethnic composition of the USA and foreign policy: on Cuba there is, exceptionally, a direct connection, the Cuban vote in Florida and New Jersey long constituting a block to any development in relations with Havana. But there is a certain convergence, an elective and electoral affinity, between demographic change and a resurgent, post-cold-war unilateralism: a shift towards the Pacific and Latin America and away from Europe, the insistent populist rejection of international institutions, a more angry note on trade and employment issues – all meet the concerns of constituencies old and new.

Interest in, and knowledge about, the outside world, never that high in any society, are, if anything, less than was previously the case in America, with the declining attention of the media, in particular television news, to what happens outside America: this is of considerable importance for the performance of an international role. Republican 2000 presidential candidate George W. Bush famously ignored the foreign news pages of his morning paper. If you are the dominant power, the hegemon, you do not have to care what happens outside. The former UN Secretary-General Boutros-Ghali, who was hounded from office by Secretary of State Mrs Albright, put it politely, comparing the Americans to the Romans: 'You don't need diplomacy if you are so powerful.' Yet this growing disengagement at the political and popular levels is offset by increased engagement at the economic. Today America trades a much higher percentage of its GDP with the outside world than was the case before: it is still, significantly, only half that of comparable OECD states, but it is rising. At the social level, migration and drugs tie American society more closely to the outside world than was the case a generation ago. Tastes also mark a change: in 1970 you sold beer by stressing it was American – Coors, Bud, Schlitz. Since the 1980s, it is 'imported beer' that attracts customers.

These changes in society are compounded by changes in politics itself, above all by a continuing tension between the Presidency and the Congress. The US Presidency has suffered more than one blow in recent decades: in 1974 Watergate marked the onset of this, with ominous consequences for the pursuit of détente, and the Lewinsky affair of 1998 added to it, even as it cast an interesting light on the nature of this polit-ical office. Evaluating the political impact of the Lewinsky crisis involves taking a wider view. Thirteen months of uncertainty, manoeu-vring, humiliation, and sanctimonious claptrap from Congress led in the end to a Senate decision not to pursue impeachment. It appeared in one sense as if this crisis had *not* affected US foreign policymaking. Throughout the crisis President Clinton had remained, in his own terms, 'focused' and 'engaged' in international negotiation – on Ireland, the Arab-Israeli dispute, Iraq. Perhaps the one case where, it can be argued, lack of attention to the detail of a fast-moving crisis may have worsened the outcome in a specific way was during the August 1998 debt melt-down in Russia: on this occasion White House attention *was* diverted. But here, and in all the other cases, there is a recurrent fallacy about American policy – its omnipotence: the notion that had the US president been fully focused, he could have solved everything. Such international actors as the IRA, Ossama bin Laden and the Russian financial mafia did not need a crisis in Washington, Monica Lewinsky or anyone else, to pursue their particular ends.

Here indeed another fallacy was very much in fashion, the anti-internationalist reflex that runs deep in US political culture, left and right: while a more persuasive critique of his foreign policy would be that it was too timid (on Bosnia, Kosovo, Palestine), Clinton ran the risk of being accused not of inaction, but of diversionary action, in cases where he did act – firing missiles in August 1998 after the terrorist attacks on US embassies in Africa, authorizing the NATO attack on Serbia in March 1999. The most facile criticism of any foreign policy action is indeed to say that it is a way of deflecting attention from domestic troubles, and Clinton's US, and foreign, critics were not slow to claim this. The film *Wag the Dog*, in which an imaginary US president launches a war against Albania to save himself from domestic scandal, caught the spirit of the moment. Yet it was a null criticism: it looked smart, even original, to accuse Clinton during the Lewinsky crisis of diversion by foreign initiatives. But what appeared smart was not so, a reflex of critics and conspiracy bores who, lacking analysis of the international system itself, fall back on the trite. Hostility to international commitments is prevalent on the conservative right – as in the rhetoric of Pat Buchanan railing against the US presence in the 3 'Ks', Korea, Kuwait, Kosovo – and calling for the expulsion of the UN from US soil. But, no one is more smug in such contexts than the American liberal, who has no wish or ability to analyse the international situation in its own terms and for whom *every* external initiative has some covert, domestic agenda. It is worth recalling the words of Gore Vidal, a good novelist who, like the obsessionally anti-American English playwright Harold Pinter, has 'gotten off' the creative reservation, during the 1990 crisis over Kuwait: 'As an American patriot, why should I worry about Saddam Hussein? He's no worse than the Los Angeles Police Department.'

These reflexes masked, rather than illuminated, the relation of domestic to international politics. A different verdict can, however, be returned not on the presidential response to specific crises, but on the way handling of relations with Congress during 1998 and 1999 affected other, more long-term, issues. The loss of prestige associated with scandal can, it is arguable, be seen as part, a significant part, of the failure to get support for some international trade agreements, to ratify participation in the International Criminal Court, and to mount a more effective defence of the UN. It certainly compounded that reluctance to engage in ground combat that characterized, and in part discredited, the US response to the Kosovo crisis. Even more so, was it pertinent to the most disastrous Congressional decision of all, the rejection by the Senate of the Comprehensive Test Ban Treaty (CTBT) in October 1999. Here, folly in the White House, and pseudo-judicial obsession on the Hill, combined to forge a climate in which the security of the world was gravely threatened. It was the failure of the president to pursue foreign policy goals, not the success of any diversionary 'tail' wagging the 'dog', which constituted the global fallout for the ongoing conflict of President and Congress.

Foreign Policy in Dispute

To these domestic changes have been added the debates about the conduct of US foreign policy. The greatest mistake to make about

America, apart from wishing that it would behave like other countries, is to treat its foreign policy debate as unitary. US foreign policy has long been marked by a set of polarized debates which have in very different contexts reproduced similar sets of views of world affairs and of America's place in them. In the aftermath of World War I, Woodrow Wilson sought to draw America into a new liberal world order, based on the League of Nations. In 1920, the US Congress, espousing what was then termed 'isolationism', rejected membership of the League, which was fatally undermined by that withdrawal. In the 1930s and up to Pearl Harbour, isolationism continued to be strong, but was gradually weakened by Roosevelt's move towards alliance with Britain against Nazi Germany. The Japanese attack in December 1941 stilled that debate.

During the cold war, there was broad consensus about the need to confront the USSR, and to sustain alliances with fellow anti-communist states in Europe and the Far East, whether or not they were democratic, but considerable disagreement about how confrontational, or how co-operative, to be in dealings with Moscow. Two camps, termed by Michael Klare the 'Prussians' and the 'Traders', emerged, the latter laying greater stress on the force of American economic power, the former stressing the continued need for US military superiority.[7] In the 1970s, President Carter espoused the 'Trader' policy, in the 1980s, President Reagan the 'Prussian'. His defence of the US-controlled, Panama Canal Zone said it all: 'we stole it, fair and square'. Each of these camps claimed its own victory when communism collapsed: the 'Prussians' ascribed their victory to the pressure of the arms race, 'we bust them by outspending them'; the 'Traders' argued it was western economic performance, in Europe as in the USA, and the Helsinki Conference of 1975, which included in Basket IV human rights provisions to which the Soviet Union was in some way committed, that unleashed the collapse of the system. Not that the issue was ever as clear as these simple divisions suggest. The proponents of geostrategy, notably Henry Kissinger, derided the Helsinki provisions on human rights and only in retrospect came to see them as important. There were at the same time often those, on the more conservative or realist side, who doubted the wisdom of global military extension. George Kennan, the theorist of containment, believed, more or less, that what happened in the Third World did not matter that much: if China or Vietnam wanted to go communist, then let it. A comparable caution was espoused by the father of American academic realism, Hans Morgenthau. Nor were alliances as cosy as pretended: Republicans were polite in public, but less so in private, about the failure of the European allies, and of Japan, to share military burdens and impatient with the allied carping at the alleged inexperience, clumsiness and lack of perspective of American diplomacy.

On the left and liberal side, there were those who, equally, doubted the wisdom of any foreign engagements: the arms race was, they argued, promoted by a military–industrial complex and by Congressmen with interests in getting contracts for their own constituency; the Soviet threat was fabricated for electoral reasons; the upheavals in the Third World were a result of US provocation and intervention.[8] In what was a left version of the isolationist assumption, the US itself, so they argued, had been corrupted by the foreign engagements and nuclear politics of the post-1945 epoch. The proof of all this was the disastrous involvement in Vietnam. However, the analysis of domestic factors was too rarely balanced with an evaluation of what was indeed happening outside – to friend and foe alike. The hostility of revolutionary leaders was not just a product of misperception or bias in Washington. Ho Chi Minh, Fidel Castro, Ruhollah Khomeini and Daniel Ortega had real reasons to confront the USA. At the same time, the confrontations Washington found itself in were not just figments of domestic hawks: there were real threats and problems out there, and, more importantly, responsibilities in the security, economic and humanitarian fields. The fulfilment of a liberal agenda is not now, nor was it ever, for America merely to retreat into itself. The easy option for liberals was to cast *all* foreign actions as imperialist. The difficult one was to elaborate a policy that used American power and influence for liberal purposes.

The dividing lines of the new millennium run along lines inherited from these earlier debates. With appropriate shuffling of the arguments, there are continuities. A full American isolationism is not on the cards, as it might have been before World War II: America's economic power is so bound up with the rest of the world that it would be folly, even on the most nationalistic of grounds, to withdraw. Now the argument arises in what is most conventionally termed 'multilateralist' and 'unilateralist' forms. Multilateralism suggests engagement with international organizations – the UN, the WTO, NATO – while the unilateralists would be more sceptical about these and would push America's interests first. As so often in US politics, many hark back to the terms of debate in the earlier years of the Republic: Thomas Jefferson, it is said, would be suspicious of what the current world commitment does to US liberties, Andrew Jackson would opt for a more clear proclamation of the national interest, while Wilsonians would espouse liberal engagement and the assumption of some enlightened burden of world leadership.

The new unilateralism is marked as much as anything by *tone*, what Khomeini rather aptly termed *istikbar-i jahani*, 'world arrogance'. Gone are the days when US Congressmen and political candidates made it a point to travel in order to prepare themselves for discussion and decision. The House of Representatives majority leader Richard Armey, from Texas, had no need to visit Europe, he had 'already been there once'. Trent Lott, the Senate Republican leader, expressed in many ways the outlook of the new unilateralists: in contrast to earlier US congressional leaders, who regularly visited other countries, Mr Lott too boasted that he does not go abroad – indeed a third of the US Congress do not have passports. Lott had openly mocked at the foreign names of his opponents in terms that are redolent of racist contempt – Michel Camdessus, the head of the IMF, and Boutros Boutros-Ghali, the former UN Secretary-General, being cases in point. Of Camdessus he once said 'He's French, and a socialist. Need I say more?' If you go to the Senator's website, it does not say 'American First' but 'Tennessee First'.

The voices of unilateralism are clear, and in some areas increasingly effective. A good example could be found in a debate between the three main Republican candidates for the Presidency in February 2000: each sought in his initial remarks to assert himself as a champion of unilateralism. George W. Bush said the USA should stop trying to co-operate with China: he would treat China as a competitor, not a partner, in world affairs. Alan Keyes wanted to tear up the 1972 ABM Treaty. John McCain wanted a policy of active 'roll-back' against rogue states. George W. Bush and John McCain had already previously espoused, in their different ways, versions of this muscular, when not aggressive, pursuit of national interest. Bush had opposed the US intervention in Kosovo, on the grounds that this was 'Clinton's war', while McCain argued for a more forceful policy against what are termed 'rogue states' such as Iran, North Korea and Iraq. Bush, in his rhetoric, touched on older themes about the USA not needing to care about foreign wars; McCain, playing on his record as a Vietnam war hero, and referring to Vietnamese as 'gooks', touched on the interventionism which is also part of the US conservative heritage.

The revival of support for the Vietnam War, embodied in such books as Michael Lind's *Vietnam: The Necessary War*, represented an important shift to a post-Clinton, less multilateralist orientation. Bush's foreign policy adviser Condoleezza Rice's phrase: 'Doing good is not a strategy', misses the point that democracy and the protection of human rights are the basis of international security. The timbre of unilateralism is heard elsewhere as well. With a voice that is wider in influence than his electoral following, Pat Buchanan, right-wing populist commentator and presidential candidate for the Reform Party, summed up his foreign policy in characteristically succinct terms: 'America, first, second, third.' Buchanan had been critical of multilateral commercial arrangements, such as NAFTA and the WTO, opposed US involvement in Kosovo, and had gone so far as to question the wisdom of US involvement in World War II. He wanted all US forces out of Europe in three years.

The unilateralist agenda is wide-ranging: resistance to environmental and trade agreements, the promotion of a new system of NMD, that would decouple European defence from that of the USA (see Chapter 4), continued harassment of the UN and other international organizations. Here defence is a token of a larger, and widening, gap between US and international opinion on political *and* ethical issues. On capital punishment, US opinion is also at odds with that abroad. Irresponsibility on the CTBT and the International Criminal Court and growing restiveness on WTO obligations combine with a broader refusal to accept international obligations. Few even bother now to argue for the continuation of what was, in the 1960s and 70s, a central feature of US and, more broadly, OECD policy, aid to the Third World: as private flows of capital from developed states to the Third World rise, to over $250 billion a year – comprising FDI, portfolio investment and private bank loans – official US state aid has fallen to 0.10% of GDP. This is a far cry from the 0.7% called for in the Brandt Report of 1980, the lowest percentage of any OECD state, and a puny proportion compared to the substantial ratios spent by Canada, Holland and Scandinavian countries – as a percentage of GDP, US aid is just one-seventh that of Sweden. An obligation on the part of the world's richest, and ever-richer, state seems to have evaporated.

The contrasted position to unilateralism is that of multilateralism: multilateralism appeals to internationalist traditions in American thought, ones conveniently buoyed by the current state of the US economy, but also draws on analyses of the contemporary world which stress that, however possible insulation may have been in the past, this is no longer an option today. Trade, IT, the environment, migration and drugs all make it essential for America to be engaged, consultative, and, within limits, co-operative. The question is not *whether* America leads but *whither* it leads.

Its most recent, if battered, embodiment, is, of course, William Jefferson Clinton. Clinton was, in ways obvious and not so obvious, an imperfect leader: some of his decisions spoke of an opportunism and lack of courage that merited condemnation. A case in point was his opposition, later overcome, to a World Bank proposal in favour of lowering tariffs on exports by the poorest Third World countries to the USA. While all can make their own lists of his failures, the full-scale indictment to which he is often treated, by conservatives and irate liberals alike, is unsustainable. Many presidents would have done less. The multilateralists, in the persons of Clinton, and his secretaries of state Warren Christopher and Madeleine Albright, sought to maintain a more consultative, and active, engagement with international institutions. Clinton stalled on NMD, tried to push NAFTA, the WTO and environmental policy, and argued for US intervention in defence of humanitarian goals in Bosnia and Kosovo.

In a major speech in March 1999 Clinton outlined his vision of multilateral engagement.[9] Globalization was, he said, inexorable, but it contained no guarantees of peace, freedom or prosperity, nor of avoiding environmental and public health crises. The US faced, he argued, five challenges: building a peaceful twenty-first century; incorporating Russia and China into the international economic system; protecting against the dangers of weapons proliferation, terrorism, drugs and climate change; creating a world financial system of benefit to all; maintaining freedom.

This was, in outline form, the multilateral agenda which would, indeed, benefit America *and* the world. Yet it was contested most from within the USA – by isolationists and unilateralists on the one side, by left and liberal doubters on the other. Yet faced with the alternatives, from within America and without, it might have appeared that the greatest danger lay in the failure of this programme rather than in its implementation.

The Limits of Hyperpower

One factor shaping the exercise of US power has, therefore, been the debate *within* the USA: too often ignored by critics, and enthusiasts, of US policy outside, it is the decisive factor in US policy formation and in limiting US ability to shape a new world order. There was, however, another weakness in the 'New World Order' idea, even for those who believed in it. This was, quite simply, that it overstated what the USA or any coalition of permanent members of the Security Council could do. The claims of US leadership and the diffused view of the USA as a most powerful state – superpower, 'hyperpower', great power or whatever – distracted attention from the reality, that any state, however powerful, faces limits.

Three examples will suffice. First, diplomatic intervention in inter-ethnic conflicts. The USA was engaged throughout the 1990s in trying to promote negotiated solutions to communal and inter-ethnic conflicts around the world: in Ireland, Palestine, Nagorno-Karabach, Kashmir, Ethiopia and Eritrea. In Bosnia and Kosovo, the USA intervened to prevent war crimes but did so belatedly and could not impose a political solution after such interventions. In some cases, progress was made, and ceasefires held, but in the latter two they most certainly did not. In none was a full, final peace settlement reached. The inter-state war of Ethiopia and Eritrea, the most serious in the contemporary world, defied mediation by the OAU, USA, EU and everyone else. The conflict in Kosovo involved both Serbian and Albanian nationalist gangsters. Clinton tried on his visit to South Asia in March 2000 to persuade India and Pakistan to abandon their nuclear policies and to negotiate on Kashmir: they listened politely and then made it clear they had paid no attention at all to what he had said. In such cases, the primary fault does not lie with the USA or other outside powers, nor with the multiple channels of mediation and NGO work that have accompanied the activity of states. Responsibility for these impasses lies with the local politicians, in and out of power. It was they who obstructed compromise, promoted hate against their neighbours, and reneged on the spirit, when not the letter, of agreements. That these problems continued was not the fault of the USA, the EU, NATO, the OSCE or any other external body. In a word, it lay with national *and* nationalist leaders.

A second example of the limits of power is that of drugs policy. Drugs are today the second largest commodity traded, by value, in the world market, at $400 billion, according to the UN, equal to 8% of world trade, second only to oil. The USA is the largest importer and consumer of drugs. Since the late 1980s, official policy has been to inhibit the supply of coca, and its refined form, cocaine: in 1989 Congress passed the National Defense Authorization Act which made the Department of Defense the 'single lead agency' in the war on drugs – a task the Pentagon was initially reluctant to take on, but which the end of the cold war, which left the US military short of legitimizing tasks, made more attractive to it. Hundreds of millions of dollars have been spent in Peru, Colombia and Mexico, in an attempt to wipe out production and processing, and interdict supply of these drugs to the USA. Yet the policy is not succeeding: whenever one area, or means of transport, is targeted, others take their place. The large cartels of a decade ago, Medellín and Cali, have now been replaced by a mass of smaller *cartelitos*.

The ineffectiveness of this campaign pales, however, before two other problems. One is that US policy is directed against the suppliers, poor farmers who earn three times as much from producing drugs as they could from any other crop, and not against those who consume: drug users are after all, along with car users, a major domestic lobby, if an unseen one, of several million in the USA itself. Displacing the problem onto the suppliers is not a solution. The US policy, of drug interdiction tied to military, and in Colombia to counter-insurgency, action and with the inevitable extradition disputes that ensue, is widely seen as a form of imperialist intervention. In Mexico, Colombia and Peru there is growing anger at the intervention, and one-sided character, of the US narcotics policy. Beyond these problems lies a broader policy vacuum. The drugs issue has been growing for two decades: in the USA, and in Europe, governments have failed, and are failing, to address it. They dither between supply interdiction and ineffective discussions of legalization. Public opinion tends to adopt punitive, and thereby all the more unrealistic, positions. Policy experts and those involved in interdiction continue to assert that they *have* solutions, and that things are going, in some way or other, to get better: in regard to this matter, one may greatly doubt it. Along with migration and the environment, narcotics are an issue not created, but certainly enhanced, by globalization and to which states have no coherent ethical or practical response.

The limits, but in this case also confusions, of US power are evident in a third respect, that of its policy towards what came in the 1990s to be termed 'rogue' or 'pariah' states, renamed in 2000 as 'states of concern'. The debate was often on how to treat such states, but it would be better to begin by questioning the terminology itself. The very category is arguably spurious, denying as it does the legit-imate national interests of the state involved, and creating an image of a world ruled by a global sheriff. Neither Iran nor Cuba has invaded any other country, nor are they threatening the security of the USA. US policy on these is at odds with the rest of the devel-oped world, a prisoner of domestic constituencies. Denunciation of Iraq is, however, more justified, based as it is on Iraq's record as an aggressor against Iran and Kuwait, and the refusal of the Iraqi government to meet UN requirements on inspection and monitoring of its weapons of mass destruction, which it has demonstrated it is prepared to use against neighbours (Iran) and its own people (Kurds) alike. To put Iraq in the same category as Cuba is ridiculous, and devalues any attempt to promote a serious, multilateral, intelligent security policy.

There is also an element of historical foreshortening at work here: the causes of today's conflicts in yesterday's aggression are too easily denied. Iran, for example, has supported terrorist acts abroad, and has played an obstructive role in the Arab-Israeli peace process. But these actions pale before what the west, Britain in particular, but also the USA, have done to that country – in the British case invading it in two world wars, in the USA and British cases over-throwing its democratically elected government in 1953, and in 1980 supporting Iraq in its invasion of Iran, at that juncture the clearest violation of the UN Charter since 1945. European policy of the 1990s, of engaging with Iran, was far more creative and informed than was the embargo on the oil and gas industries authorized by the US Congress, through the Iran–Libya Sanctions Act of 1996. US policy towards Cuba is equally short-sighted: there has to be, and there will be, a process of democratization in Cuba, but it is not helped, but rather hindered, by the US embargo.

The temptations and luxury of hegemony mean that the USA is in danger of becoming more and more detached from a responsible world role. Its own political culture and leadership are ambivalent, at best, about multilateral engagement. At the same time the limits, domestic and international, on US power mean not only that there is no 'New World Order' as a co-operative international venture, but that, to an increasing degree, the world may not be subject to US political or strategic control. The balance of power is most certainly not a factor in the contemporary world, even as the proponents of this theory lengthen the time-frame in which some rival power, or power bloc, could emerge to challenge US hegemony. What may develop, however, in parallel with US unaccountability is a growing, if unfocused, resentment outside the USA which takes issue not only with US military intervention as such, but also with the impact of US policies on a range of issues, from IT to human rights. This is an opposition which sees a hegemonic, indeed imperialist, intent wherever US action or influence is felt and denies, on its side, the possibility and benefit of multilateralism. A new world will not, therefore, replicate the old, in creating a power bloc to challenge Washington. Rather a globalized resentment, based on issues false or not so false, threatens to create a rancorous world that US power will be unable to control, even as the USA turns more and more to unilateralist irresponsibility.

The USA and the World: Towards a Balance Sheet

The uses to which American power is put will be decisive for the future of the world as a whole. At the moment the USA is, within the limits identified, predominant, and is likely to remain so. Under his successors, as under Clinton, Washington is going to pursue its own interests, with its allies if it can, against them or independent of them if it cannot. We see this in the increasing, and possibly disruptive, divisions over international security, as we do in the debates within the WTO or the administration of the World Wide Web, where European users challenge the hegemony of ICANN. Here it is possible to suggest where some limits on US power, and the transition to global unaccountability, may lie. It would be desirable to see a reduction, marked, committed, sustained, in the arrogance of American power: a Congress that listened to the rest of the world and made it its business to find out; US media, printed and electronic, which paid sufficient attention to the outside world; a US film industry that did not seek in its greed to trample on the creations of other cultures and studios; a US e-mail regime in which the USA too had to use its own addressing suffix; a US political and business culture that accepted the rulings of the WTO instead of moaning and backsliding on its adjudications. It would be good to see the back of the ayatollah of isolationism Senator Jesse Helms, as the world saw in 1996 the back of Senator D'Amato.

In recognizing, and resolving, the ever-present legacy of the cold war it would, above all, be apposite to hear a more balanced discussion of Vietnam. The USA lost 58,000 men in Vietnam: no one who visits the Vietnam memorial in Washington, a dignified dark slab lying partly below the ground, can fail to be moved, least of all if they are of the generation of those who died. But we need to hear less on what Vietnam did to America, a moratorium on talk about 'an American tragedy' or a 'quagmire', as if the US involvement was no one's fault, and more on what the USA did *to* that country, killing an estimated 3.8 million people and devastating much of the environment. The place to start is not with American reflections on the pain it suffered, *The Deer Hunter* or *Apocalypse Now*, but with the Vietnamese writer Bao Nink's *The Sorrow of War*.

US power is not only an enduring but, if properly used, potentially positive feature of the global system. It should be the aim of those who wish to make that system more generally prosperous and more just to work with those in the USA who have a similar outlook. Multilateralism and what in the USA is often termed 'internationalism' are far from dead and, indeed, often take, what to Europeans appear to be, utopian and inflated forms – witness campaigns to ban under international law the possession of nuclear weapons, or to open security services to public scrutiny, let alone the 35,000 'ruckus-makers' of Seattle. Part of any multilateral engagement from without is to find common causes with those within, even if it is also to dissent from, and, on occasion to temper, the wilder forms of conspiracy theory and oppositional response to which radicals within the USA too easily resort.

Underlying this whole debate, as it has done since the eighteenth century, and pertaining to both olive tree and Lexus, is the issue of values. The political language and values of America have their own particular history and resonance: there is no other way to understand the US debate on taxation, or capital punishment, or gun control, all retrograde issues rooted in political culture and now sustained by special interests. But this political language is, in the main, one shared, with the Europe from which it originated, and with the rest of the world which has now been incorporated, by a mixture of subjugation and choice, into the global system. The values of democracy, independence, pluralism, economic prosperity and, most significantly, rights in their political and social dimensions are ones espoused, even as they are differently interpreted, the world over. The USA has, for all its imperialism and inconsistencies, played an important part in defining, redefining and promoting these, and could continue to do so. Indeed, much of the radical culture of the modern world – from the Declaration of Independence, through May Day and the protest movement of the 1960s – originates in America.

America has had, and will continue to have, an important place in these debates, as a power and as an intellectual stimulant, but the end results, the definition of rights, and the degree to which they are realized, are ones in which the rest of the world has its own, diverse role to play. The world of the twenty-first century cannot be fashioned without America, nor should it be fashioned on America's terms, especially when these are defined in a selective, hegemonic manner. Faced with the predominant or indispensable power, neither rejection nor adulation provides an answer. In a post-cold-war world, the debate can be not only between America and the rest of the world, but within and across borders, between rival interpretations of global issues.

8

Delusions of Difference

There is no global survey of world culture, akin to *Fortune 500*, the *Strategy Survey* of the International Institute of Strategic Studies or the UNDP's *World Development Report*. Yet a brief look at the state of world culture today would, at first sight, suggest great vitality and change: a world of over 10,000 spoken languages; a boom of both traditional forms of publication, such as books and newspapers, and new electronic forms of communication; an explosion of creativity in music, architecture, design. The means of communication – global media and everything associated with them – are growing in reach as new technologies come to the fore, even if, as with so much of the contemporary world economy, within an oligarchic form. For those inclined to see religion as an important component of culture, it too appears to be on the rebound – in the USA above all, and in the Muslim world, the link between secularization and modernity seems to be more and more attenuated. We have no global secularization index, but it would appear in some countries to be falling, or at least not continuing to rise. As for identity, community, ethnicity, there is no limit to their moral, and financial, claims. The global and the particular seem to prosper in counterpoint.

No one familiar with international politics at the start of the twenty-first century can be unaware of the importance placed on 'culture', meaning in a political context systems of belief about community and society and, not to be ignored, the implications of these for international relations itself. Those who write on the post-cold-war world, and on the impact of globalization, have much to say on this issue. Here too the twentieth century has bequeathed its vibrant, and in some cases virulent, bequest. As with so much of what characterizes the discussion on the contemporary world, the disagreement may be as much about historical depth, about the novelty of current developments, as it is about the trends themselves:

not all that appears tribal, primordial, atavistic necessarily is. Disagreement may also concern the degree to which that which is preserved as historically distinct really is either so historical or so distinct. 'Culture', notoriously one of the most difficult of all terms to define in social science, including international relations, is not new but has underlain much of previous history – be it empires, religions, trade routes, wars. We need to make a hard, rather than an overstated, claim as to how it matters now.

If we ask how and why all this affects international relations, then we can come up with several different answers, and several claims about the modern world. First, culture in a broad sense is said to be much more important for relations between states and peoples. Nationalism is, it is claimed, *the* dominant prevailing ideology in the world today, as an idiom of protest but also, as in the USA, in Japan and perhaps increasingly in parts of Europe, as one of asserting power and interest. The mistake in too much discussion of nationalism is to focus on just the nationalism of oppressed or protesting peoples, not on the nationalism, imperial in some degree, of powerful peoples. English concern with 'foreigners' and Japanese with *sangokujin* merit as much attention as Third World animosities. Second, we hear that international relations are becoming more and more dominated by cultural conflict, that 'Clash of Civilizations' which Samuel Huntington popularized and which nationalists and fundamentalists the world over are so eager to endorse.[1]

Third, we read that within globalization the impact of culture, and the interaction of cultures, is a process parallel to the exchanges of goods and services that lie at the core of globalization as an economic process. Indeed one of the most challenging questions in globalization is that of assessing in what ways this leads to a greater unification and homogenization of culture, and how much to greater diversity, through fragmentation, creativity or rejection of the dominant. The argument outlined in Chapter 1, about the creation of an international mythology as a form of rejection of the global, suggests that culture will be as much a site of conflict as of co-operation. At the same time, this argument about culture and the international is matched by one about domestic politics and society – here too identity, community, tradition have, it is said, become more important and legitimate. Writers on areas of inter-ethnic conflict, such as Ireland or the Balkans, are often quick to evoke the 'primordial'. Finally, we have the ethical challenges posed by this; the division of much debate within the international and domestic spheres into those who are broadly respectful of this diversity and wish to take it as a starting point – variously described as communitarians, relativists, nationalists indeed – and those who hold to a universalist aspiration, one in which, while there is diversity of cultural forms, the values, and the legal and political norms associated with them, are more universal. These are the issues which this chapter addresses. It may not help with short-run misrepresentation, and in the long run there is little to say: culture is, however, central to the intermediate time-frame, over which we may have some critical regard. It is, indeed, rather more conjunctural and less eternal than its proponents often suggest.

Those who make claims in the name of culture assert that in some way this is a given, something inherited from history, or tradition, or society which itself defines both what is, and what ought to be. Culture and tradition have, in this perspective, an independent authority. It can be argued, however, that in every case what matters is not this history, or lack of it, but the *contemporary* significance with which a symbol is invested. The music for that symbol of American patriotism, the Star Spangled Banner, was written by an Englishman, John Stafford Smith. The flag of St George, which came to be much displayed in England in the late 1990s, was named after an obscure fourth-century saint who died in Palestine. His cult, and the flag, probably reached England during the Crusades, and April 23 was designated as his day in 1222 by the Synod of Oxford. That he has nothing to do with England, never heard of the place and never went there means little, nor does the fact that he is the patron saint of several other countries, including Finland, Norway and Greece. The fact that the English, almost alone in the world, do not have a national day, but rather two birthdays for their monarch, adds to the curiosity of this case.

Flags are indeed extraordinary forms of symbolism: in themselves they have no meaning, they are just designs on a piece of cloth, just as words are mere phonemes. The red flag, for example, has had many meanings – the flag of piracy, of communism, until 1970 of the slave-owning Sultan of Muscat. The cult of the flag of St George has much to do with contemporary English dislike of Brussels and Scotland, less to do with the Middle Ages. Today flags have become symbols for broader conflicts: think of the rage which the flag of the newly independent Macedonia provoked in Greece, because it appeared to embody expansionist claims, or the row in the USA over the Confederate flag which flew over the State House in Columbia, South Carolina. This pertains also to other symbols of difference and contention such as language, religion and dress. It also applies to that which has become, in modern times, but was less so in the past, the central object of contention, namely territory. It is not territory that tells people what to do, but people who invest it with a meaning. Rocks, rivers and mountains no more *have* a national character than the moon, or holes in the ground.

This is not, of course, how things appear to most people in the world, for whom these symbols have, and have always supposedly had, an intrinsic value to which they are devoted. Nationalism and religion make claims in the name of symbols: they exert authority over people, and send them to fight others, in the name of such iden-tities – land, flags, crosses, crescents and so on. But it is not just retrospective nationalists and proponents of religion who give to cultural and allegedly traditional differences such importance: we are living in a period when across a broad spectrum of opinion, among politicians, secular intellectuals, and, not least, political theo-rists, the universal and the rational are questioned in the name of loyalty to the particular and the communal.

Here the claims of the particular, and of tradition and community, are given greater weight. This weight, moreover, has two sides – not only an ethical weight, in terms of what we as individuals ought to do, but also an analytic or explanatory weight, in terms of how we explain social behaviour within countries, and relations between peoples and states. The contemporary world, particularly the world since the collapse of communism, is one in which ethnic and cultural differences have returned: the primordial, the atavistic and the tradi-tional are re-exerting their hold; the repressed are returning; a new nationalism is emerging. We hear much about 'deep structures' and, in a related trend, with the growing acceptance of sociobiological approaches that seek to explain human behaviour in terms of genetic inheritance and innate behavioural traits, an increased emphasis on the importance of borders, conflict, and antagonism in human behav-iour. The history of individual peoples, and indeed of whole conti-nents such as 'Europe', is now being written in terms of a cultural formation defined by something outside, 'the other'. This cult of difference is seen not as an alternative to globalization but as part or even a result of it. Together with this renewed attention to culture in the historical formation of peoples and states, there is a growing attention to the role of the cultural in changing and shaping the new post-modern transnational and global world – the very speed of informational and cultural interchange, and the rise of diasporas promote a greater intermixing and impact of culture.

A prime example of this contemporary usage of culture as a form of explanation is Professor Samuel Huntington's 'Clash of Civilisations'. Huntington argues that we can divide the world up into six or seven major cultural zones, or civilizations, and that increasingly international relations will be determined by relations between these. The conflicts of the coming era will be cultural, as other ideological distinctions recede. Holding to the view of international conflict as inevitable, itself a dubious proposition, Huntington has, in part, a residual argument; 'If not culture, then what?' he says. Pride of place in this world view is ascribed to the clash between the Islamic and western worlds: 'Islam has bloody frontiers' he proclaims, the implication being that, wherever there is a clash between the Muslim and non-Muslim worlds, it is Islam, seen as a coherent political entity, which is at fault. But arguments analogous to Huntington's have much wider diffusion. In the Far East, instead of Islam, China or 'Confucianism', or 'Asian values' can be substituted. Such views are espoused as much by liberal, and critical thinkers, and by a range of post-modernists, as they are by the exponents of traditional or 'realist' conflict.[2]

It is, however, possible to take issue with this approach, to offer an alternative view of the role of culture, and religion, in the contemporary world. We may have given far too much ground, in definition and explanation, to those who espouse such arguments as we have to those who ascribe ethical import to community and identity. Much of this is bad history, bad sociology, and bad international relations. It may also be bad ethics. What can be termed 'fault-line babble' has come to be the intellectual malaise of our time. As with the flag of St George, we need to have an informed history and sociology of how culture changes and interacts with other phenomena, to be sceptical about the moral claims made in their name. The point about territorial conflict is not that any piece of rock or forest has an undisputed, or historically, prime owner, or that a piece of cloth with some arbitrarily designed pattern has sacred properties, but that modern states, and nationalists, have made a fetish of them. Too often we find other concerns, not least power and interest themselves, lying behind the apparent injunctions of culture.

A Necessary Sociology of Knowledge

The first place to start is with the questioning of culture and civilization as givens. In one of the most famous of all works of historical sociology, Barrington Moore's *The Social Origins of Dictatorship and Democracy*, published in 1967, the author writes as follows:

> Culture or tradition is not something that exists outside of or independently of individual human beings living together in society. Cultural values do not descend from heaven to influence the course of history. To explain behaviour in terms of cultural values is to engage in circular reasoning. The assumption of inertia, that cultural and social continuity do not require explanation, obliterates the fact that both have to be recreated anew in each generation, often with great pain and suffering. To maintain and transmit a value system, human beings are punched, bullied, sent to jail, thrown into concentration camps, cajoled, bribed, made into heroes, encouraged to read newspapers, stood up against a wall and shot, and sometimes even taught sociology. To speak of cultural inertia is to overlook the concrete interests and privileges that are served by indoctrination, education, and the entire complicated process of transmitting culture from one generation to the next.[3]

Barrington Moore invites the reader to ask at least two questions. The first is, how ideas, symbols, cultures are transmitted. One cannot deduce the present from the past, nor can one, as is rather too common, transpose valid insights into how an individual is shaped by his or her past, and particularly their childhood, to the history of collective entities, such as nations or peoples. If an identity, or language, or animosity holds today it is because it has been in the interests of someone to continue it. When a Frenchmen says to me tetchily '*Mais, vous avez bien brûlé Jeanne d'Arc*' (But you burnt Joan of Arc at the stake), he is saying something about an airline ticket queue, or a football match, or the BSE disease transmitted by cows, or the intrusions of the English language into contemporary French, not what happened at her trial at Rouen in 1431.

In the Middle East, much is made of the past, and of the ancient animosities of peoples: but these are continued, or revived, or selected for present purposes. During the Iran-Iraq War, Saddam Hussein used to refer to Khomeini as a *magus*, a Persian or Zoroastrian priest, and his battle against Iran as Qadissiya, the battle in 648 when the Arab Islamic armies defeated Iran. For his part, Khomeini used to refer to Saddam as a Yazid, the name of the Ummayad caliph who killed the founder of Shi'ism, Hussein bin Ali. Both accused the other of going to Tel Aviv every week to get their instructions, something one has reason to doubt. Interesting variations of diatribe can be noted here: in the Mediterranean Arab countries, once known as the Levant, western aggressors are termed *salibiin*, or crusaders, but this is not the term Saddam used when the USA and its allies attacked Iraq in January 1991: then he denounced them as 'Mongols' and US President George Bush as Hulagu, the Mongol ruler who sacked Baghdad in 1258.

The continuity of identity, and animosity, depends on the mechanisms of reproduction that Barrington Moore identifies. In Britain it may take a relatively harmless form – history textbooks, names of streets and pubs, the *Sun* newspaper on a bad day. The *Sun* has indeed published a book, *Hold Ye Front Page*, which it hopes to place in every school in Britain, with invented chauvinist headlines for English history as a whole. In the Balkans, this takes a more lethal form with television and music denouncing other communities, and transmitting a history of hatred and paranoia. It was the modern media, in the service of modern states and leaders, which ensured that the same thing happened again. The reason 'hate-speak' is needed is because hatred is not self-perpetuating: it depends on people to transmit it.

Barrington Moore also invites examination, as does much of the sociology and history of nationalism, of how a particular past is constructed. The essentialist, nationalist or religious answer is that there is one past, one culture, one tradition, one 'true or', a key word this, 'authentic' identity. The argument then becomes what the true identity, or tradition, is. But this is not how things are. On the one hand, the past is not one text, or message, but many: it is, to use a metaphor from gastronomy, and as are the texts of the great religions, not a fixed price, but an à la carte menu. The best exemplar of this is language: we inherit, and live in, languages with meaning and rules, but we are in large measure free to say what we want within them. Structure does not obstruct, but may actually facilitate, agency. We choose what we want from the varied records available – and the choice is dictated by contemporary interests, and concerns, not by what is given in the past. If you want to use your national traditions, or religions, to prove the validity of monarchy, you can do so, the same for republicanism. Every religion can, and has been used, to justify a variety of socio-economic forms – not just socialism or capitalism, but feudalism and slavery too. Tolerance, and intolerance, slavery and individual freedom can all as easily be derived from core texts.

In the Arab-Israeli context, we can see the uses to which holy texts are put: among Palestinian Muslims, those who favour a peace with Israel cite the example of the *hudna* or truce signed by the Prophet with non-believers; those against cite verses of the Koran enjoining struggle against the infidel. On the Jewish side, the argument has revolved in part around the question of whether a Jewish state can give away Jewish land: those against territorial concessions say you cannot, those in favour cite the story from the scriptures whereby King Solomon gave away land to the King of Sidon. When it comes to gender relations, and the position of women, a similar variety of interpretations is possible. We select, define and ransack the past for what we need, just as in our own accounts of ourselves as individuals we choose those bits of our past that are most pertinent to present needs. A university, when celebrating its centenary, highlights those alumni who bring it renown, not those who might be redolent of scandal or subversion. Every nation salutes its great heroes, not those it chooses to forget; the Ukrainians do not celebrate the most famous Ukrainian of all, Leon Trotsky from Kherson, or the second most famous Dr Leopold von Sacher-Masoch from Lvov, formerly Lemberg, who first described the condition that bears his name. The third most famous, Chmielnicki, is remembered as a nationalist rebel, not as what he also was, the most famous anti-Semite before Hitler. The English choose to forget the eighteenth-century radical Tom Paine. There are few, if any, pubs named after this most famous and influential of English writers, although there is a good ale, brewed in Lewes, Sussex, that bears his name. The statue to Paine in his home village of Thetford, Norfolk, was paid for by American servicemen stationed near there during World War II.

The contemporary formation of tradition and culture goes further than that. Beyond selection, amnesia, and reformulation lies invention itself, the pretence of antiquity for that which is not. This 'invention of tradition', in the words of a famous work, applies equally to religion as to nationalism.[4] The role of invention in nationalism is well known and its examples legion: from the kilt of the Scots invented in the 1820s, to the 'ploughman's lunch' of the English, a pub snack fabricated by an advertising agency in the 1960s. The combination of selected and invented past is evident everywhere. The English chose as the anthem of their 1998 entry to the World Cup a song about chicken vindaloo, an Indian, or more precisely Goan, dish, itself probably named after the Portuguese for 'welcome' *bem-vindo*. In 1995 the ambassador of one former Soviet republic, invited to contribute its 'national' flower to a fiftieth anniversary of the defeat of Nazi Germany in London, chose its entry from a mail order catalogue.

A striking example of the varying origins of symbols is to be found within the Jewish tradition. One of its core symbols, the candelabra or *minora*, is indeed of ancient origin: it can be seen on the walls of synagogues as at Katzrin in the Golan Heights from nearly two millennia ago. The other core symbol of Jewish identity, the Star, or literally 'Shield' of David or *magen david*, is not an ancient Jewish symbol at all: it has nothing to do with the historic King David. A hexagram symbol of the unity of all being, it was used by mystical writers of all three major religions in the Middle Ages. Only in the late nineteenth century did it come to be a symbol of specifically Jewish identity. On the Palestinian side, perhaps the most widespread symbol is the red *keffiyeh* or headdress: the traditional Palestinian Beduin headdress was dark blue or indigo, and the red version was designed in the 1920s by a merchant family in Manchester, originally Sephardim from Aleppo, who had received a commission from the British government for the new Jordanian army. By the 1970s it had come to symbolise Palestinian nationalism. None of this affects the validity of, or affect associated with, these symbols today or the legitimacy of the political claims made in their name.

The same selection by modernity may be found in fundamentalist religion. The Taliban in Afghanistan claim that they are waging a war on images of living beings in the name of Islam: films and photographs are banned, there have even been public smashings of TV sets. The television is *sunduq-i sheitun*, 'Satan's Box'. But there is on closer inspection nothing in the Koran that forbids such images: the Islamic prohibition, closely intertwined over the centuries with similar trends in Judaism and Christianity, rests on two sayings or *hadith* attributed to the Prophet. The Catholic obsession with the celibacy of the clergy and the loyalty of Jewish orthodox or *haredim* to the dark hats and long coats or *kapota*, which are those of an eighteenth-century Polish squire, are equally constructed. It is not antiquity, or authenticity, but current definition that determines the uses and

associations of these symbols. When it comes to two other repositories of the authentic, language and food, even more selection, and
invention, occurs: words are regarded as genuine or not, food is
national or not, based on the flimsiest of criteria. Perhaps nothing,
other than ancestry and kinship, is as contingent.

Transnationalism in Context

The claim of historically constituted cultures, civilizations,
languages, ethical systems is one pillar of the argument for cultural
conflict and civilizational incompatibility. The other is an argument
from history – that these blocks, like the blobs of colour denoting
countries on a map, have been there from time immemorial and, by
some combination of history and nature, and perhaps divine will or
providence, represented natural entities. More specifically, as far as
Huntington and his fellow thinkers are concerned, these cultures
have always been in conflict and will continue to be so. Neither of
these propositions holds up. The peoples, religions, cultures of the
world have distinct compositions, and are in some measure distinct
today. But over the centuries they have interacted, perhaps more so
in the past than they do now: it is the modern state, not ancient
community, that has parcelled out the world. If one looks at the
origin of the three monotheistic Middle Eastern religions, one can
see that their theology, texts, values have a common source. They
have continued to interact over the millennia. Food is equally
porous: no historic, as opposed to contemporary, validity applies to
English cooking if it includes potatoes and tomatoes, pepper and the
ingredients of Lee & Perrins sauce, all brought from across the
oceans by the developing world market of recent centuries.

This interaction may, in addition, help to set in context something
that is too readily seen as peculiar to the modern or post-modern
condition, the movement of ideas and symbols across frontiers. Here
we see a good example of the short-sightedness, or conceit, of much
contemporary discussion. Modern communications do certainly
permit a rapid and voluminous transmission of cultural material
around the world. But it is the rapidity and volume which are new,
not the phenomenon itself. If we take the great religions, then they
spread, if not with the speed of a computer, but with that of a horse
or a sailing ship. The ideas of Christ, and Mohammed, and of count-

less preachers, saints and heretics were transmitted around the Mediterranean world. When Martin Luther fixed his 95 theses, denouncing the sale of indulgences, to the door of All Saints Church Wittenberg on 31 October 1517, CNN was not there to record the moment: but within a few years his ideas had contributed to a major upheaval throughout Europe. In the eighteenth century, the ideas of European political thought informed debate in the Americas, just as American radicalism affected Europe. The same applies to another defining characteristic of contemporary cultural and political analysis, that of hybridity: the assumption here is that hitherto identities were unitary, and discrete, and that it is only in modern times that this changed. But hybridity is recurrent throughout history – with no disrespect to their faithful, all great religions are syncretic, borrowing themes, symbols, dates and forms of ceremonial from their multiple predecessors and, once established, imitating even as they contend with, their opponents. The Christian halo is a relic of earlier sun worship. The history of, say, iconoclasm, or holy war, in Judaism, Christianity and Islam is one of borrowing and imitation, amidst rivalry. The same applies to language. A Dutch philologist once expostulated to me: 'You English speakers don't have a language. English is just a bastard creation of German and French.' He was right, but this bastard has been the vehicle for great human creativity and amusement. Long may it continue.

In politics too, the picture is fluid. If we look at the pattern of inter-state relations in modern times, or earlier centuries, they do not follow cultural or civilizational boundaries. The Ottoman Empire is conventionally presented as the great non-European 'other' against which Europe defined itself. In Austria the nationalist Jörg Haider has chosen as one of his heroes Count von Starhamberg, who defended Vienna against the Turkish siege in 1683. Yet the Ottoman Empire was not engaged in constant conflict with European powers. It allied with France and Britain against Russia in the Crimean War, and with Germany and Austria against France and Britain in World War I. In the twentieth century the most ferocious wars were between states, and peoples, of the same cultural bloc – France, Britain, Russia and Germany in Europe, Japan and China in the Far East, Iran and Iraq in the Middle East. If anything, it is what Freud termed 'narcissism of small differences', rather than inter-civilizational or inter-cultural conflict, the 'narcissism of large differences', which has constituted the world of today.

The Misuse of the 'Other'

Beneath this picture of cultural conflict lie two other, deeper, assumptions, both of which merit being identified and challenged. One, already questioned in the quotation from Barrington Moore, is that of the determination by the past of the present. Talk of the 'returning' repressed, the primordial, the substratum assumes that which it sets out to prove. The past *may* influence or determine the present, but even in individuals, let alone in collective entities, this needs to be argued for rather than assumed. Where present interest is masked by the recourse to the past, then the attribution to the past should be questioned. It is not only nationalists or the faithful who do this, but also the supposedly most radical and innovative of all political actors, revolutionaries: the twentieth-century revolutionary looked back to 1917, the Bolsheviks looked back to the French Revolution, the French revolutionaries to ancient Rome. Khomeini, of course, looked to Mecca and Medina, and the Prophet, in the seventh century. But all that claims derivation or authority from the past is not so easily explained by that past.

There is a further assumption, in the writings of Huntington, as in those of so many others who comment upon the post-cold-war world and its conflicts, that in some way confrontation, conflict, the identification of an enemy are essential and enduring features of political and social life. This may take the form of Arnold Toynbee's historical theme 'Challenge and Response', it may take the form of contemporary analysis of the role of the 'other' in the formation of national, and broader civilizational, identity. In this context, anthropological work on boundaries and identity, and sociobiological work on animal behaviour and genetic selection play their part. In this neo-Darwinian age, it is easy to go down such a track. There is, obviously, validity in the claim, rooted in history, of confrontation with the external as a stimulant to internal change: it is true of individuals, who mature through facing tests, and it is true of societies.

This, however, is a contingent claim, not a necessary one. The opposite may also be true: individuals may be overcome, or traumatized, by challenges and may, by contrast, be encouraged to grow through love and support. Similarly, societies may be stimulated through challenge, but they also may be inhibited by external confrontations. Nor is external challenge a necessary precondition for human development. The physical growth of individuals has nothing to do with external challenge, everything to do with endogenous growth. If we look at some of the major processes of modern history, the same applies: the creation of new societies in the Americas, one of the most momentous transformations of the past half millennium given subsequent evolution, was not carried out against any external enemy – pre-Colombian Americans did not threaten Europe, or the European colonies established in the New World. The Industrial Revolution was only in part a result of external pressure, more of endogenous growth and opportunity. The Internet has not met an external 'other', but has been generated by enthusiasts.

When we come to the contemporary, post-1989 world, we hear much about the need to create new challenges to replace the communist threat. Threat inflation by those with a vested interest, financial and bureaucratic, in continued funding for conflict is one such resort: the Pentagon is not slow to engage in this. Those who view the international arena in what are termed 'realist' categories also assert this – this is the theoretical charge behind Huntington's question 'If not culture, then what?' But we can detect a broader argument, latent in much of the discussion about the Middle East and China, and their relations with the west, about some basic need – societal, ideological, strategic, it is not clear which – to find a substitute enemy.

The most obvious candidate, as far as the west is concerned, and one which Islamist fundamentalists are not slow to offer themselves, is of course 'Islam'. But the premise itself needs examination. Not only is it questionable on historical grounds, but it is also questionable as an account of recent world history. Communism, in its effective lifetime from 1917 to 1991, did tend to exaggerate its challenge to the west, while, at the same time, engaging in denial that it presented any challenge at all. All revolutionaries exaggerate: they shout about how they are going to change the world, with the helping hand of a determinist history. All of that aside, communism *did* challenge the west: it appealed to many millions around the world, and people fought and died for it. In the inter-war period, when western democracies and economies were collapsing, communism appeared to offer a superior economic alternative – a claim that was widely held, by friend and foe alike, into the 1960s. The Soviet leader Khrushchev's boast to the west 'We shall bury you' alarmed as much as it inspired. At its height, after World War II, the USSR presented a strategic challenge to the west in the nuclear field, and in the wars of Asia and Africa its forces mounted an effective, and deadly, conventional military challenge. It is false history, and by extension a false analogy, to claim that *since* communism was 'invented' as a threat, consequently that of Islam, or some other post-1989 threat, is equally invented. Communism was not invented, it was real enough, whatever the exaggeration on both sides. No post-1989 challenge comes near to filling that gap. The 54 Muslim states are not a coherent economic or military unit and compete with each other as much as with the rest of the world. Nor is there any need for the Muslim world to do so: the argument about the necessary 'other' fails the tests of history and the contemporary world alike.

Beyond Cultural Conflict

Against this background, it may become possible to assess the place of culture and cultural conflict in globalization. Culture has come to occupy a special place in the discussion of globalization that is itself worldwide. Whatever happens to war or the international economy, here at least it might seem that we can indeed retain an argument about conflict and its generation for the coming century. Yet it may be that this apparent link between globalization and cultural conflict is misleading: and that it is largely because politicians and writers, in developed and underdeveloped societies, are invoking it that it may acquire a reality as the myth comes to determine political behaviour.

As this chapter has suggested, other factors may, however, be at work. On the one hand, culture has become not the residual source of conflict, but the residual appeal for political legitimacy – aspirants to power, or those who wish to confirm their existing power, resort to it as a way of mobilizing support. The source of the conflict lies not, therefore, in the diversity of conflicts, but in the competition for power within and between states, something that is certainly not going to go away, whatever happens to globalization. At the same time, there is, beneath an apparent flowering of difference, a modular process in train that is making societies more homogeneous: globalization itself, indeed the whole history of the internationalization of social and political forms over recent centuries, reinforces this. For example, every state has to have certain attributes – a capital, a flag, a national anthem, an airline, a national football team, a national dress, a national food. Each presents itself as different, yet the genesis is the same. The example of legislatures, as of national airlines, is suggestive; each gives itself a separate name, invoking something from the national past, but it is the pressure for similarity that drives the production of distinct names. Bundesrat and Sejm, Knesset and Majlis, Congress and Dáil, Parliament and Duma speak to a different past, but are shaped, indeed demanded, by a similar present. In the case of national airlines, be it Aer Lingus, Aeroflot, El Al or Lufthansa, this had better be even more true, given the consequences of flying in the face of the laws of aerodynamics and air traffic control.

At the same time, an emphasis on cultural diversity may mask the power of more material forms of difference. Culture may conceal the reality of other issues that are very much in dispute but which the rhetoric of globalization itself obscures, most obviously, differences of economic interest. Countries whose primary products' prices are dependent on developed states, or whose exports are prevented from competing in developed markets, have real grievances. The rhetoric of Ayatollah Khomeini and other Islamic fundamentalists is as much about underdevelopment, unequal trade, arms purchases and the imposition, real or imagined, of autocratic regimes on their societies. Cultural rejection is a form of resistance to domination, yet by concentrating on culture it may divert attention from the other, political and economic, inequalities that reinforce that domination.

The logic of globalization in its economic and political forms is not to promote, but rather to ignore, differences of culture. In some respects, globalization promotes a more homogeneous world, and a destruction of those differences that make for human diversity. But globalization is also compatible with a variety of languages, religions and cuisines, because it is precisely in the contemporary world that these do not matter. The global elite being forged by business and finance is drawn from the whole world: it has a shared lifestyle and idiom, but within that differences of culture subsist. It was Voltaire who said in the sixth of his *Lettres Philosophiques* over two and half centuries ago that capital was blind to religious difference:

Go into the London Stock Exchange... there you will see the representatives of all nations assembled for the benefit of mankind. There the Jew, the Mohammedan and the Christian treat each other as if they were of the same religion, and they give the name of infidel only to those who are bankrupt.[5]

9

Governance Beyond Frontiers

In his engaging *Dictionnaire du XXIe siècle*, Jacques Attali suggests that 'fraternity' will be the great utopia of the coming age.[1] The end of the cold war and the advance of globalization have given a significant impetus to discussion, and speculation, about global institutions that further such collaborative interaction. Just as classical liberal concerns about democracy would appear to have received a new lease of life from the end of the cold war, so aspirations to creating international institutions and a broader sense of international responsibility have similarly been reinvigorated. As with democracy, this involves the refurbishment of ideas that have their own history. A little short of eternal life or perpetual motion, but a long way away from the mundane constraints and difficulties of actual politics, indeed there is no topic more likely to spur the imagination of thinkers or to foster projects that enthusiastically override the constraints of the present than the creation of a global or world order. Such projects have both a political and a social or cultural dimension – they aspire to *internationalism*, in the sense of a politics that addresses a global rather than a national interest, and to *cosmopolitanism*, in the sense of the creation of a community that embraces the whole world. The record of history is, however, decidedly two-sided: for all that history reinforces aspiration, it also serves to provide warnings of the difficulties, and some dangers, involved.

Internationalism in Flux

The aspiration to a broader and more coherent system of international co-operation and, indeed, to the creation of a single world political, cultural and ethical community has inspired politicians and thinkers for centuries. Such a goal long predates the emergence of the modern world system, let alone contemporary globalization. All great religions have exhibited, in their positing of a universal moral code and the identification of a community that is larger than the nation, elements of such cosmopolitan thinking, even as they can, equally, be used to legitimate national and violent states. The European Enlightenment, while equally liable as a set of ideas for use by rulers and by nationalists, also promoted an internationalist vision. In 1784 Kant speculated about the possibility of a cosmopolitan order, while in 1817 Goethe announced the end of national literature and the advent of a world literature.

Throughout the nineteenth and twentieth centuries there was no shortage of plans for a world political order, and of optimistic sightings of its onset. The death of nations, of nationalism, of particularist association and of individual national or state interest was enthusiastically proclaimed. The term much used from the 1970s onwards to denote these processes, 'interdependence', was being used in the 1840s. *The Manifesto of the Communist Party* of Karl Marx and Friedrich Engels, published in 1848, contains passages on the unstoppable spread of markets, and the unification of the world, that read at times like publicity material for the World Bank. No political tradition could claim a monopoly of the internationalist vision, which could be found in three broad variants – a liberal, a hegemonic or imperial, and a revolutionary.[2] Liberals spoke of the growing import of trade, of communications, of reason itself in fostering co-operation among nations and states; conservatives concerned with order were keen to ensure that the authority of states, and the capacity to control nationalist challenges, was strengthened by international links; revolutionaries, from France in the 1790s to Iran in the 1980s, dreamt of throwing down frontiers and forging a new world community of the oppressed.

All of this has, certainly, been given new impetus by the revival of globalization. The growth of communications, trade and other contacts between peoples has, it seems, brought the liberal vision of a global community all the nearer. New waves of mass migration, the formation of ethnically diverse cities in the developed world (Sydney, Berlin, Paris, London, Montreal, Los Angeles) even as others are ethnically homogenized elsewhere (Saigon, Bombay, Tehran, Baghdad, Alexandria), the emergence of new forms of cultural 'hybridity' within migrant communities all appear to contribute to this forging of a new, more unified, world. In the field of social relations and culture, globalization is marked by forms of cultural syncretism in language, food, dress, music and by the erosion of identity in terms of loyalty to a particular nation state. Tourism moves larger numbers of people across the world: around 700 million per year in 2000, a figure scheduled to rise to 1.5 billion by 2015.

At the same time and in myriad ways, globalization is fostering a new politics. It creates the *need* for greater international co-operation – be it in constructing a 'financial architecture' to regulate the world economy, in intensified air traffic control requirements, in common taxation policies, or in regulating the environment. At the same time, the power of individual states is being eroded, and forms of international co-operation, between states, and transnational linkages, between social movements, NGOs and other elements of civil society, are growing, leading to the use of the term 'global civil society'. Easier travel and the possibilities of communication provided by the Internet allow not only those with power but those without to communicate, mobilize and consult across frontiers and continents. In legal and ethical terms, the growth of international codes of rights and good practice, the challenging of state sovereignty through UN conventions on human rights and through various forms of humanitarian intervention suggest the possibility of a normative system that is, in aspiration and to some degree in practice, international.

Globalization, therefore, creates both the possibility and the need for international co-operation: finally, it would seem, the internationalist hour, of Attali's *Fraternité*, has struck. All three of the historic forms of internationalism can recruit the present to vindicate themselves: liberal internationalists see globalization as having produced the processes that will realize their vision of co-operation; hegemonic internationalists can see the triumph of American power, finance and technology as vindicating their vision of a stable world order; revolutionaries see the need for, and possibility of, a global 'anti-hegemonic' mobilization against the industrial capitalist system that they see as oppressing humanity and destroying the planet. Each has found its own millennial message to declaim. 'Our resistance must be as global as capital', proclaimed protesters in Seattle.

It is, however, not quite so easy. The very fact that internationalist and cosmopolitan projects have been thought of for so long without success may give pause. A number of classic problems persist. First, it is often not clear how far what is presented as an international interest is in fact the interest of a particular state or group within the international system. Second, there endures a tension between the aspiration to a global culture or identity and the existence, and value, of diversity: a world in which everyone spoke the same language or ate the same food would be dull indeed – a global vista of dark suits and black dresses is bad enough. Third, the creation and sustaining of any international order involve resources and political will, something often lacking, not least as the challenges of globalization promote nationalist responses. Finally, while advocates of internationalism call for greater co-operation to realize common goals, it is not always evident that an 'international interest' can be identified, in the sense of a course of action that will maximize benefit to all: peace does not always favour the oppressed, equality does not favour the privileged, few vote seriously to reduce the role of the car.

History also provides caution. The fate of internationalism of all three broad kinds tells its own tale: liberal internationalism of the nineteenth century led to World War I; today it is facing increasing opposition from those who see it as a hegemonic, western, and particularly US, imposition. The hegemonic internationalism of the European empires collapsed after World War II, that of the USSR in the late 1980s, that of the USA may face the same fate. The revolutionary internationalism of France, Russia, China and Iran led to war with their neighbours, and to a fierce nationalism and repressive state building at home. The diverse anti-capitalist and protest movements of the 1990s and beyond, from radical ecologists, anti-capitalists and Chiapas guerrillas lack an organizational cohesion that would challenge the powers of states and corporations that they denounce. All that is transnational, moreover, is not necessarily cosmopolitan. Diaspora politics are marked not so much by identification with global values as by ferocious pursuit of the interest of their own sectional interest. Cross-cultural sexual interaction, xenophilia, is prone to narcissism. The tourists who flock to other countries may absorb the language and culture of their places of destination but may equally inhabit a cocoon of national displacement. For perhaps as many as a million women and children who are forcibly trafficked across frontiers each year, as sex workers or manual labourers, transnationalism is far from being a benign process.

The aspiration to abolish differences between states and nations has, therefore, been at once recurrent and ineffective: in the context of globalization it has arisen anew, yet so too have the objections to it. In a world that is marked by large and growing inequalities, any internationalist project promoted by states may give the appearance of being a guise for domination: the same suspicion of an imperialist internationalism applies to the power of multinational corporations as it does to the domination of the English language. In trade, the environment and the provision of medical care globalization strengthens special, national and corporate, interests. At the same time, the state, the historic core of power and legitimacy, retains, as we have seen, much of its hold on the lives and aspirations of peoples. National languages and identities continue to flourish and are in some measure fostered by the impact of globalization. We continue and shall continue to live in a world of diversity, in politics and in culture: we do not have an internationalist order, let alone a cosmopolitan one, but rather one of diverse, if increasingly co-ordinated, states and cultures.

Here lies the relevance of what has, since the early 1990s, come to be termed 'global governance'. 'Global governance' lies short of internationalist idealism, but a degree beyond a world of constant competition. It rests on an international system of states, with a shared set of values, about the independence and sovereignty of states on the one hand, and the significance of political rights within them. The tension between these two is long-standing, and is clear within the UN Charter: but it has been accentuated by the end of that great power rivalry that characterized the cold war and which contained concern with rights and domestic orders. In a very real sense, the new international situation has sharpened that conflict, leading to a much greater emphasis upon rights and democratic procedures *within* states. To this extent, it has contributed to raising the aspirations which are held about states and the governance system.

This very heightened expectation and the increased demand made of governance have, however, also necessitated a more realistic discourse about what governance can do: the greatest mistake to make is that of believing that such bodies are either all powerful, or its members motivated solely by the highest of principles. In discussion of humanitarian intervention, for example, it is easy, but mistaken, to argue that states should only act when they have no interest: this would be a recipe for complete paralysis of the governance system. In regard to the role of UN bodies or NGOs in crisis situations, it is equally unrealistic to accept that they are either all-powerful or staffed by the most incorruptible of personnel. UN peacekeeping forces uphold the wishes of the Security Council and stop people killing each other. They may also engage in smuggling operations, stimulate prostitution rackets, and defraud their headquarters through selling arms, fuel, medicine and food to local protagonists.

High-minded perfectionism is, therefore, as much an enemy of an effective global governance system as is one that dismisses this system as ineffectual, or an interference in the otherwise supreme interests of states. The double revision in global governance occasioned by the altered international system is one of accepting a much greater conflict of sovereignty and universal normative principles on the one hand, and a reduced, less angelic, view of the workings of governance on the other.

The Advent of 'Governance'

The term 'global governance' itself has at least two distinct sources. One is that it represents a rethinking about how international organizations should be established: in contrast to the earlier goal of global 'government', something that was united within one single system, 'governance' is meant to imply that the management of world affairs is distributed across a range of institutions, some with distinct competences, some with overlapping responsibilities, some organized by states, some by private business co-ordination, some by NGOs. For example, in regard to security in Europe there are now numerous inter-governmental bodies that share, or purport to share, responsibility – the UN, NATO, the EU with its Common Foreign and Security Policy, the OSCE, the Council of Europe, the Western European Union, Partnership for Peace and, more recently, the Euro-Atlantic Partnership Council. In the management of the world economy, the World Bank and the IMF are, at least officially, part of the UN system: but other bodies that have come to play an influential role are not – the annual summit meetings of the Group of 8, an informal but influential gathering, the Bank of International Settlements, more recently the WTO, not to mention myriad specific regulatory bodies.

Global governance suggests not only this kind of diversity but also a greater depth than might have been present in the idea of a single supranational authority, embodied in the UN. Regional organizations, NGOs, local government, the media are all seen to have their role. In the regulation of the world economy, much of the formative work is done by private entities: the management of foreign currency transfers, for example, is handled by Swift, an independent co-operative, owned by banks, based in Brussels; the rules for global accountancy are set by private co-ordination; insurance rates are equally a product of private negotiation and regulation. Just as within states the effectiveness of government at the centre rests on a range of formal and informal supportive mechanisms, so the survival of global governance requires much more than the support of states.

This rethinking of the organizational form of international institutions is one source of the term 'governance'. The other lies in a shift of mood or ethos about these institutions themselves, in particular a greater scepticism and an abandonment of that liberal optimism which was earlier associated with the UN and associated bodies. Here governance means good practice, accountability and transparency, rather than a set of bodies run by unaccountable officials and riven with corrupt practices. The impulse for this may have come from a changed private sector management ethos of the 1980s and 90s, but the institutions of global governance themselves have provided plenty of targets for criticism: immobilism, overmanning, inflated budgets, verbose and ineffective conferences, appalling treatment of women (staff and spouses), ramshackle – when not corrupt – promotion and career structures. In large measure, of course, these practices at the international level reflect national practices of member states and of influential representatives and nominees of those states: but the very offshore or international character of these institutions allows a further measure, a surcharge of inefficiency, to enter the equation. This has itself accentuated the widespread scepticism, a democratic deficit, from which many such institutions suffer.

Not all of the criticism of international organizations comes in the form of management reports: some take a more abrupt, at times brutal, form. In the field of peacekeeping, the UN found itself, in the 1990s, faced with a growing disregard worldwide for its authority and goals. On the ground, local militants attacked, killed, took hostage and otherwise abused the peacekeepers sent into their midst: in a range of countries, from Lebanon and Bosnia to Angola, the UN had to watch as local forces rampaged in violation of UN resolutions. Other elements in the governance structure, including many NGOs, and even the International Committee of the Red Cross (*not* its representatives insist an NGO but an international organization), have seen their envoys manipulated, kidnapped, or even murdered in conflicts around the world. In some countries, notably Somalia, Rwanda and Bosnia, the UN's mission was destroyed by the opposition of local forces. But this disparagement from below was to a considerable degree compounded by disparagement from above: states, particularly the USA, refused to pay their dues to the UN; appeals for support for peacekeeping by Secretaries-General were ignored. Boutros Boutros-Ghali, Secretary-General from 1990 to 1996, was restrained, but clear, in his denunciation of the role of states, above all the USA, in weakening his effectiveness in office.[3] Given its limited resources, it did not help either that the UN was treated as a talking shop by delegations who, in the General Assembly as in many specialized committees and agencies, declaimed in windowless halls without heed to practicalities or resources. As critics often, and rightly, point out, problems are not necessarily solved by holding conferences about them. In this context, governance requires a closer fit between the organization's goals and its capabilities, and a reduction in the gap between those sections of the UN, and the global governance system more generally, that are devoted to talking, and those that are capable, and willing, to act.

Anti-imperialist critics, in North and South, are at times prone to denounce this whole system. The alternative to weak, bad, or corrupt governance is not, however, to abandon it: global governance is, whether we like the term or not, here to stay. Three obvious areas that make this clear are human rights, peacekeeping and global financial management. It is easy to show how inadequate have been the sets of institutions which have emerged in each case and how special interests, of states, corporations and other lobbies, have influenced outcomes. Yet the UN Commission on Human Rights, the International Criminal Court, the Security Council and the peace-keeping forces it has mandated, and the institutions of the IMF, the World Bank and cognate bodies can be used, or changed, to reflect a programme of global reform. The challenge is not to throw it all out the window, nor is it to reject the possibility of regulation. For example, if the human rights regime represents imperialist or ethno-centric particularities, and interests, then it should be reworked to be more equal and less self-serving. If the rules proposed for invest-ment or trade are one-sided, then there should be rules that are not – but not no rules at all.

Mention has been made of the difficulty of identifying a 'global' or 'international' interest. Two of the most pressing international issues, where it may or may not be possible to recognize such an interest, are migration and the environment. In regard to the former, the only alternative to chaos and rising resentment in both labour exporting and labour importing states is some sort of regulation – that is, negotiations, plans, agreements between states. The International Organization for Migration and the International Labour Organization are designed to perform that very task, something states have not as yet allowed them to do. In the environment, there have already been several major international agreements at Montreal, Rio de Janeiro and Kyoto: the problem with them is not that they seek to regulate environmental practices within states, but that their powers to enforce treaties do not go far enough, and that the agreements themselves are insufficient.

Governance: Four Levels

Global governance is not, therefore, about creating stronger supra-national bodies in opposition to the societies and states that comprise them: if they did they would soon fail. 'Governance' invokes, rather, a system of multi-layered authority and policymaking: today, more than ever, we can see the system of global governance as based on four distinct levels. At the top lie international organizations, such as the UN and the EU. Below them lie the traditional repositories of political power and democratic legitimacy, states. Below these lies civil society in its broadest sense, within countries and between them: this comprises NGOs and social movements, but also the press, religious groups and all who seek, without assuming the authority of state, to influence its activities. Finally, and too easily forgotten in an age of structures, communities, global trends and so on, there is the basis of the whole story, the individual, all six billion plus of us.

A model of what a workable, democratic system of global governance would be is not difficult to imagine. Much of its rests on that realm of predictable, undramatic development of co-operation which has underlain the growth of international institutions over the decades since 1945. The journalistic term, 'dull but important', sums this up. It would involve effective, negotiated functioning of international institutions and efficient relations between them. States would support, fund and implement the decisions of these organizations. Civil society would work with both international institutions and states, within a democratic and legal framework. Individuals would be both informed about, and committed to, the functioning of the system as a whole. To a degree, this can, and does, work. The growth of international organizations, regulatory bodies and the mass of NGOs is spectacular. In western and now central Europe in particular, the growth of the EU is a striking example of international co-operation backed to a reasonable degree by states, civil society and individuals. Communications, travel and the very transnational character of many problems hitherto conceived of in restricted terms have encouraged the growth of a community of specialists and officials with international competence. Dull but important this may be, it is much of the stuff of governance and regulation.

Yet here, as in so much of international affairs, the desire for reform can easily slide into the promotion of myth. To each of these levels of global governance – institutions, states, civil society, individuals – there corresponds a degree of misconception. These stalk the current discussion of global governance and its interrelationship with globalization. I would like to mark out four issues on which a degree of scepticism and concern is in order.

The first concerns the durability of the governance system: there is no reason to think it can, or will, continue indefinitely. Elements of anterior governance systems survive: diplomatic practice was codified in 1815, the Anti-Slavery Society began operating in the 1820s, the International Postal Union dates from the 1870s, the International Labour Organization – the only surviving component of the League of Nations – from 1919. Yet previous general systems for managing international security did not prove immortal: the Concert of Europe, established at Vienna in 1815, ceased to function in a formal way in the 1820s and petered out in the decades that followed; the League of Nations, established at Versailles in 1919, had ceased to be effective by the early 1930s.

The system of global governance of today has been built up mainly since World War II. It has managed security, trade and much else besides. It has done much better than its predecessors, but it is not in the best of shape, in part because of the increased tensions within the changed international context on the one hand, and the greater complexity of the transactions that require regulation on the other.

From below, there is widespread scepticism about, say, the EU – and not just in Britain where it is particularly prominently reported. There is, let it be emphasized, nothing inevitable or final about the EU: it too is a human institution. It sometimes looks as if the EU has become the beneficiary of the new idealism. After the notion of a transition to socialism, long delayed but widely believed in, we now have the transition to a united Europe. It may happen, but it may not. We should note, but beware of, a free-floating tendency to idealize the present in the name of the future, as if there is a 'Single Transferable Utopia' that was locked for some decades around the construction of a socialist order and has now been reallocated to European integration. If we are asked to think forward a decade or two for new academic programmes, I would open a file, a small one at the moment, on 'The Fragmentation of Trade Areas'.

For its part, the UN is, as we have seen, defied and abused as much as it is respected. UN peacekeeping, for example, was in confident form over the Kuwait crisis of 1990–91, but took a steep dive thereafter – in Somalia, Rwanda, and Bosnia. The UN's policy of sanctions provides another example: long favoured by liberal internationalists as an alternative to war, or at least providing a breathing space for diplomacy to be effective, it had, by the late 1990s, come to be seen as a hegemonic, when not brutal, option rather than as a desirable form of political pressure. Under the impact of the sanctions on Iraq, distorted by the Baghdad regime to appear as the result of external rather than their own, internal, punishment of the Iraqi people, liberal opinion swung away from sanctions as an instrument: a perhaps naive belief in their use being replaced by an overly absolute rejection of them as a policy. Other institutions, notably the IMF and the World Bank, have also come in for their share of criticism – from right and left.

Second, there is the cornerstone of the system, states. The international governance system, as the international economic system, is necessarily driven and defined by its more powerful states. The question is not whether this is desirable or not – in many ways it is not – but whether that power will be used in a more or less responsible manner. The greatest challenge facing global governance is indeed this issue – of whether, as in 1914, international co-operation will be destroyed by unilateralism and inter-state conflict. The myth of the Seattle protests of late 1999 was that somehow a network of global protesters stopped the WTO in its tracks. The Seattle conference failed because the states *inside* could not agree on what to do: the Europeans could not agree with the Americans, the Third World states such as India, Brazil and Egypt could not agree with the OECD states. That was the main game in town, not the 30,000 protesters on the streets.

In particular, all major international institutions require the commitment of the strongest state of all, the USA: yet, as examined in Chapter 7, the USA is ambivalent about the whole structure of global governance, wishing to influence it, without accepting either its responsibilities or its obligations to comply. The future of US policy towards the international system in general, and towards the UN in particular, will be one of the major questions of the coming decades.

When we come to the third level, that of global civil society: a similar caution is in order. There is something that can legitimately be termed a global civil society: a network of NGOs and liberal groups like Amnesty International, Greenpeace and Oxfam who are pushing governments and public opinion for change. On certain issues – debt relief, anti-personnel mines, the environment – global civil society has made a major impact. Education, travel, the Internet, social interaction itself have produced a global elite of younger people who share similar values and lifestyles and who underpin the culture, and practice, of globalization. But, as already discussed in Chapter 3, the powers of civil society, separate from states, should not be exaggerated. While NGOs can, on occasion, challenge multinationals, they can do little to alter patterns of investment and employment worldwide. NGOs can protest at violence and militarism, but when the killers get to work civil society is too easily swept aside – as was evident in Northern Ireland and the Basque country after the late 1960s, or Bosnia and Kosovo more recently. Moreover, an element of caution about the claim to be civil is needed: criminals have been as quick as anyone else to take advantage of globalization and the reduction of state control of frontiers. In transnational relations, as within states, all that is non-state is not liberal: the Mafia, the drug traffickers, religious fundamentalists and anti-immigration groups could all claim to be part of global civil society. NGOs are as liberal, democratic and civil as the causes they support and the internal governance structures they espouse. Most importantly, global civil society cannot replace the democratic and effective work of states. While states are influenced by civil society, the latter cannot substitute for it in terms of political decision, or regulatory power, let alone the provision of security.

A major illustration of the ambivalent character of civil society is given by the media. The media play a particularly important role in influencing civil society, and in the formation of opinion with regard to international issues. Historically, it has been the media which, as the 'fourth estate', have fulfilled the responsibility of challenging power, both that of states and of centres of authority within society. The implication of this is that, in a more globalized world, the role of the media should be enhanced, to make it a constituent of the broader structure of global governance. There are indeed several respects in which this has already to some extent taken place. The national media within any one state not only cover international issues but on occasion have acted to promote particular policies for, or against, action and intervention by that state. At the same time, and as part of globalization, the media themselves have become internationalized, through the sale of international newspapers, through satellite and cable television, before that through the activities of international news agencies.

It is, however, debatable how far the media do contribute to the workings of global governance: the spread of 'international' media acts too often to mirror hierarchies of inequality in the world economy; the campaigns of the press and TV for and against state action are often fickle; the overall tendency for the media within developed countries to be *less* concerned about international issues, and more with the apolitical and the domestic, has undercut their ability to play a responsible, indeed any, role within global governance; the horizons of public curiosity have shrunk, and been shrunk, in the post-cold-war epoch. This is the globalization of Murdoch and Berlusconi. In the USA, news and current affairs analyses have increasingly been subsumed into the 'entertainment' industry: agreements between media conglomerates and on-line providers offer even less guarantee of independence, or investigative initiative; the fallacy of digital TV is that it seems set to provide a flat diet of news, without the resources, commentary or trained correspondents that broadcasters historically have provided. In some countries, of which the UK is a prime example, much of the media promotes hostility to global governance as well as promoting, in headline, content and tone, a reproduction of low-key but resilient resentment towards other peoples and liberal principles in general. If the media are to be seen as part of the global governance system, then they must be held to account in terms of the responsibilities which accompany that system: to date, they are a failure.

It is on the decisions of individuals, their level of education, knowledge and responsibility, and on their ability to co-operate and act that the whole edifice rests. Radical critics of contemporary western democracy, such as Habermas, have called for the reconstitution of a public realm, where, without recourse to inhibitions of collective or ideological attachment, citizens may contribute to political life. Those who advocate global civil society take the argument further, to encompass international and transnational public realms. This is indeed the precondition, as well as the opportunity, for individuals, as citizens of each country and participants in whatever opening global civil society provides. If they are not supportive of the higher levels, if they are not informed by a critical and adult press, if their assumptions about politics, domestic and international, are not tested, and their idols challenged, then the whole thing will come tumbling down. It has happened before, and it could happen again.

10

For a Radical Universalism

No discussion of the world at 2000 can avoid an analysis of values, global and national, about how people, individually and collectively, judge the present and what they aspire to in the future. In this regard, there are two great illusions that haunt contemporary debate. One, to which we were treated in excess over the millennium itself, is that utopianism is dead. It is as if we could hear a sigh of global relief, that the age of ideologies, of extreme views, of alternatives was over. Now we are entering a period when a sensible, managerial consensus can prevail, where all problems can be calmly addressed. Francis Fukuyama has argued that, in the sense of the exhaustion of ideological conflict over fundamentals, history is over. François Furet, in his autopsy on communism, has stated that, for the first time in 200 years, humanity does not have an alibi, there is no glorious, alternative future in the name of which the present may be rejected outright, and humanity be called to make radical or revolutionary sacrifices.[1] They mistake a point of method, the possibility of reasoned debate, with one of substance, the end of major differences of value. The second great illusion is that of relativism, the argument building on the role of culture that, in relations between states and societies, shared values are not possible. Here there are two variants, a 'relativism from above', promoted by states who wish to fend off international criticism, and a 'relativism from below', by those who see universalism as a threat by powerful forces outside their own society. Each of these illusions, the end of utopia and relativism, merits attention in its turn.

The Need for Utopia

As discussed in Chapter 3, there is not a vision in the world today, both radical and influential, of what an alternative society could be.

Few now aspire to go forward to a communist society of the kind that many millions of people fought for in the twentieth century. Residual areas of support subsist: members of some radical movements around the world – the PKK, *Sendero Luminoso*, some residual if vocal protagonists of Trotsky's mantle, some of the many millions in the former communist countries, whose lives have suffered as a result of what is naively termed 'the transition' – hold to a future defined in revolutionary terms. They are, however, not in a position to command widespread support, in any country, let alone to shape the course of international relations. The residual communist states – North Korea, Cuba – are on the verge of dramatic change. For its part, China has, despite its retention of one party rule, long abandoned the claim that it represents a global alternative.

Some argue that we do have alternatives, in, for example, nationalism or Islamic fundamentalism. But these may be discounted for much the same reasons that Fukuyama gives. None posits a social or economic organization radically different from the liberal market model upheld elsewhere: one of the most striking silences of religious fundamentalism is its lack of any project for a distinctive *economic* programme. In ideological terms, there is also less difference than may appear: nationalism and fundamentalism have at their core a set of modern categories and goals – political power, economic development, a legitimacy that is, if not democratic, then at least demotic. The language, the symbolism, the cultural heritage invoked may be different, the substance is not. Nationalism may orient people to a distinct sense of the past: it cannot do so for the future, for two reasons above all else. One is the pressure to integrate into the world economy, the other is the need to allow migration: the former entails that there can be no 'national' path of economic development, the latter promotes a wish by large numbers of people to leave their own country and seek advancement in another.

The idea that the world is rid of radical choices, that it has exhausted its potential for alternatives, is not new: it has itself a long history, going back to the eighteenth century in European thought, and to much earlier periods in the paradises, places without history, of religion.[2] It was, of course, also an assumption of completion that characterized the world's empires: the British, French, Dutch and before them the Romans and the Chinese made analogous assumptions about the durability of their orders. Belief in such finality was equally the abiding illusion of Soviet communism and its imitators:

history had produced an outcome, a movement beyond the capitalist present, that could not be reversed. Under communism various 'problems' – women, nationalities, housing, crime – had been 'solved'. It did not prove true then, nor, one may surmise, will it prove so in the capitalist future. Such 'solutions' are a characteristic illusion of hegemons, and as subject to challenge and change as much as any other such illusion. The return of insecurity to the streets and rural areas of developed states is one example of such a reversal, the predicted spread of new forms of epidemic across many parts of the developing world may be another. There may, therefore, be scant attention paid to rethinking the contemporary international system, but it is an illusion to pretend that this is neither possible, nor desirable. Without such a rethinking, without, indeed, a note of impatience and concern, matched to a realism of outcome, we are not going to navigate this century or address the issues the world faces.

The argument that we now face an orderly, managerial future, without radical alternatives, is fundamentally flawed in other respects as well. First of all, we should remember the observation of the most renowned 'realist' thinker of twentieth-century international relations, E.H. Carr. All politics, he emphasized, has to combine realism, the awareness of power, and utopianism, the aspiration to a different world, the denial of the given in the name of something different, imaginable if also unattainable. It is not a matter of choosing one or the other but of managing the tension between the two.[3] Thinking about alternatives is not a contingent, let alone aberrant, feature of modern politics, an early mid-life crisis which beset modernity in the twentieth century and through which we have now, mercifully, passed. It is, rather, a recurrent feature of the human condition itself: expressed earlier in religion, it has, in the past two centuries, taken a political and social form. Marx was right when he said that religion was 'the sigh of the oppressed', and right to draw attention to this continuity of human aspiration.

Yet Marx was, in another respect, mistaken: for he believed that utopias could to a considerable degree be realized. 'Mankind always sets itself only such problems as it can solve', he wrote. More convincing, perhaps, is the argument made recently by the sociologist Zygmunt Bauman that, if anything, the opposite is the case – that each generation *had* to set itself goals it could *not* fulfil, that utopia was something that necessarily pushed against reality.[4] A society that does not have utopias is like an individual who does not dream: and if creative dreaming is not permitted, then the same aspiration will, in individual and social terms, emerge in another, more deformed and destructive, manner. Sociologists have, for some decades, been surprised at the forms of rejection which an apparently all-encompassing modernity provokes: communes, religious sects, vagrancy, drug addiction and the like. In the international sphere, we may see the same destructive alternative vision – a utopianism that is itself without outcome, or emancipatory purchase, linked, in many cases, to a set of conspiracy theories about oppression and agency.

Second, there is not just a human, anthropological tendency to posit utopia, but also a philosophical need. This is the core of Bauman's work and it is one of pervasive import for international relations. Yet this philosophical need brings with it a responsibility – if, on the one hand, this involves the rejection of the given, the dissatisfaction with the agenda of power, it also entails a responsibility to posit those alternatives and rejections which free humanity, not those which plunge it from an unhappy present into an even more unhappy future. There is little point in calling for the abolition of the state, money, or trade if the alternative is a return to barbarism. If aspirations are formed either by fashion, or by the wishes of those with power, then humanity as a whole is impoverished. It is equally irresponsible to denounce the present in the name of an ideal that is unattainable, not now, but in any plausible future, let alone to persist in doing so in the name of a view of history, and an alternative political project, that history itself has shown to be futile, at best. There may be good reasons for denouncing the World Bank, the WTO or Human Rights Watch, but not in the name of unattainable ideals – be it the reconstitution of the sterling zone, or the transition to socialism.

A responsibility of critique has to be matched by a responsibility of plausibility. Here the distinction offered by W.G. Runciman between the 'probably impossible' and the 'improbably possible' is of wider and more contemporary relevance: the challenge in this apparently flat post-ideological world lies in advocating the improbable to meet Runciman's criterion of possibility.[5] Faced with the threats to peace, economic prosperity, equality and rights, there is a need to think of a future that is beyond current conventions, beyond the platitudes of those in power, yet that remains within the realm of what is possible. Two centuries ago, the abolition of slavery in the Americas was improbable, but possible: it happened. A hundred years ago the same could have been said of the ending of the European empires. Fifty years ago it could have been said of the construction of the EU or the elimination of certain fatal diseases. That all of these could be reversed does not detract from the realization of the improbable that they represented.

Third, while it may be that the world today is without the *manifestations* of alternatives and utopias, it is far from lacking in the *causes* of these challenges. Here, of course, lies the greatest fallacy in the contemporary global complacency, one enhanced conveniently by the treatment of the last century as an epoch whose convulsions are now behind us. For the majority of those who have retrospectively commented on the communist experience, it is seen as indeed an aberration: a 'God that Failed', an 'Illusion', a 'Great Disaster'. All this may be true: the failure of communism was not just contingent – a result of a poor economic record here, a loss of nerve by Gorbachev and his associates there. It was a necessary one, in its own terms and in the context of the very competition with capitalism that it had set itself. But this is not enough: we have to ask *why* it happened in the first place, what it was that drove millions of people, over most of the decades of the twentieth century, to struggle and die for that aspiration. The conventional culprits will not do: anti-democratic or Asiatic political cultures, the treachery of counter-elites, the corrupting role of intellectuals. It was the development of the modern world itself, in its vicious, warlike and frequently undemocratic character that created communism, that drove people forward into that utopia.

The tensions of that world have far from exhausted their potential to provoke, and to exploit. In changed form perhaps, many of the elements that underlay the contradictory modernity of the twentieth century, which produced the upheavals of Russia, China, Vietnam, Cuba, Iran, are with us today: economic inequality is wider than ever, the sense of global disenfranchisement, in economic and political terms, and expressed in conspiracy theories, is pervasive. The rapid spread of urbanization, such that the peasantry as a global majority disappeared at some point in the 1980s, has produced new conditions of squalor, insecurity and inequality. In the past century, capitalism did not produce its own gravedigger, as Marx had anticipated, but it did produce the very social movement which challenged it on a worldwide scale. To avoid the same thing happening again, and being needed again with or without a conscious ideology of revolt, we need to envisage a world that addresses the underlying causes of this unequal world: the oppressed are, to paraphrase Marx, still sighing, and more loudly than ever. Despite the recent resurgence of religion, there may not be enough of it to divert them.

To deny the relevance and the causes of that contested past is to be false to the present in another way, namely, as explored in Chapter 2, to deny how we get to where we are. It is easy, from the emplacement of a set of liberal democratic and prosperous countries, from, as it were, the comfort of the OECD armchair, to see the path to contemporary society as a smooth one, and disregard the unfortunate deviations as we went along. It is, of course, quite inaccurate: the violence of the past – in wars and revolutions – was as much formative of the present as was enlightened, steady progress. The rights that are proclaimed today did not fall from the trees, from the heavens, or from the tables of the powerful: they came through social and political challenges, in the American and French Revolutions of the late eighteenth century, and in the conflicts within all major countries that followed. The independence of the majority of countries in the world was not always there: it required nationalist struggles, and a growing dissatisfaction within the colonial countries themselves, to bring it about. The societies, parties, states of the OECD are where they are and what they are because of successive challenges: to forget that is to deny not only a formative history, but also the origin and extent of the unfinished agenda which those who first challenged authority within these societies advocated.

There is, therefore, a need for a perspective on international relations that is both realistic and critical, one that advocates change on the basis of what can plausibly be said to be possible, and which denies durability and legitimacy to that which exists at the moment. The challenge set by E.H. Carr is to combine realism with the advocacy of alternatives, with utopianism. Those who criticise the existing system have to do more, often much more, to show how what they are proposing is itself possible. Those who advocate the inevitability of problems have to demonstrate more effectively why they cannot change. Therein lies the means to overcome the first of the two major illusions of contemporary debate about values.

Bases of a Just Order

Here it is possible to suggest three principles that can guide such a perspective: equality, democracy and rights. These are not 'revolutionary' in the sense that the term was enthusiastically espoused by radicals these two centuries past, nor are they ideals that are unattainable. They do, however, arise out of the revolutions of the past two centuries, notably those of America and France. They constitute a programme that would, if pursued, radically transform the world yet fall into Runciman's category of the 'improbably possible'.

Equality allows no easy managerial, post-ideological solutions. In international relations, it involves the equality of states and peoples, acknowledged in international law and diplomacy, but far from recognized in practice: post-imperial arrogance on the one hand, and the arrogance of current hegemonic power on the other prevent this, as do multiple other forms of arrogance found in every region. Moreover, equality comprises that of individuals. This latter is something that challenges the authority both of states, which often fail to uphold it, and communities, ethnic and religious; their respect for the individual rights of those who are not within their own community as well as for those who are is limited. Equality sits uneasily with other ideological trends. It is a principle that is universally espoused *and* rejected: it is espoused by all cultures and states, rejected by all nationalisms for whom the superiority of their own people is implicit.

Democracy, as already discussed, has been consolidated in a range of countries, by no means the majority, and, even where it has, it is subject to challenge, a long-term erosion whose consequences could be most serious. The economic, social and cultural prerequisites for democracy necessitate as much attention as politics itself. Linked to equality, it entails, however, a fundamental conflict with that other principle of organization which has been so dominant in recent years, the market: the power of money and the ideology of consumer preference are not adjuncts to, but, as discussed in Chapter 6, distortions of, the democratic process.

The most important of all principles on which a non-idealist alternative can be built is that of rights. This is a category which is at the moment much acknowledged, above all in the range of human rights instruments enacted through the UN.[6] It is also something that has been most creatively applied to issues of social and economic development in the work of those, such as Amartya Sen, who have restored to economics an ethical dimension that it has too easily shed.[7] Within the body of human rights instruments, are not only those pertaining to political, economic and social rights, but also those pertaining to women's rights, and rights of racial equality. Contemporary discussion of rights also comprises the various Geneva Conventions on war, including those of 1977 that bind non-state actors, guerrilla and revolutionary groups, to a measure of humane treatment. Across the world, those who struggle for their rights as nations, in liberation and guerrilla groups, are sometimes quick to deny basic humanitarian treatment in war, to enemy soldiers and civilians alike. Objections to such an approach are far from dead, as rights have not only been denied but their validity much disparaged: from communitarian and other critics has come a claim that rights lack philosophical foundation and are in some way the creation of a rationalist or hegemonic project; the revolutionary left, in power and without, far too often adopted a cynical, brutalized rejection of this concept, except where it suited it for tactical reasons.

A reaffirmation of the importance of rights involves, arguably, three deeper intellectual shifts. First, it involves ascription of responsibility for their protection to society as a whole, as well as to the state: here society is not something inherently positive, civil, waiting to play its role, but a much more divided and conflictual arena. The expansion of rights conventions has been accompanied by a major shift in those held to account for their implementation of rights, one tenaciously resisted the world over: this is to move from a focus on the violations of rights by *states* to one that includes both states and *societies*, the latter comprising society as a whole, family, religion, and indeed that much vaunted term, 'community'. Where state ends and society begins may be hard to identify: that they combine, and often collude, is beyond doubt. Second, it involves recognizing the imperfect, but workable, distribution of power in the contemporary world: we cannot deny the application of criticism because those making it are part of the hegemonic bloc. If no state acts for purely altruisitic reasons, a measure of a reasonable combination of principle and interest has to be shown. Third, a reaffirmation of rights involves, for left and right, a rethinking of history: for the right, the impossibility of change has been an obstacle to, not to say an alibi against, a commitment to promoting a rights agenda, indeed any humanitarian agenda; for the left, history has provided a comforting set of 'stages', to which all else is subjected and which has, at the margin, and a very wide margin it was, justified indifference or worse towards human rights violations. Those who are at a historically more advanced stage are, even if more brutal and economically catastrophic, somehow more 'progressive': hence, in recent times, the appealing contrast between the 'anti-imperialism' of Saddam Hussein and the 'feudal' character of Kuwait. That Kuwait was no more feudal than the Soviet Union was capitalist is not the only problem, although it is one: the problem lies with the assumed historical schedule itself.

It is in this context that we can, both realistically but with a sense of a substantial alternative, think about the ethical challenges facing the international system. What this entails is that a programme that sought to generalize, enforce and sustain the three principles enunciated above is not only far from being realized, but would, if so realized, constitute a fundamental change in the contemporary world. Here it may be objected that such an approach is too superficial, too accommodating: another, more radical, challenge needs to be made. Yet the failing of the 'revolutionary' alternative as conventionally, indeed traditionally, conceived is that it not only posits an unattainable alternative but also denies the radical potential of other, just as alternative, critiques. A world in which the differences of wealth within and between peoples had been radically reduced, in which education and the growth in prosperity and science was broadly equally available to all would be fundamentally different from that of today. It is possibly, implausibly so, but possible nonetheless.

This rights agenda, as that of democracy discussed in Chapter 6, is one that is sustained not only because its goals have not been met, but because it is itself inexhaustable, and because society itself and the challenges to rights are changing. Here too there is no finality, no irreversible emancipatory attainment. The contemporary world provides new opportunities, but also new challenges: advances in IT threaten privacy; advances in biotechnology challenge ethical standards and occasion new forms of inequality in medical provision.

Two striking contemporary areas of both advance and new challenge are the rights of workers and of women. Amidst all the clamour about rights, subsidiarity, and devolution in the contemporary world, we hear almost nothing about the rights of employees, long a traditional concern of the trades union movement across the world. The phrase 'outdated labour practices' is a euphemism for the denial of rights to decent working conditions, security of employment, and restrictions on working hours for which millions fought over previous decades. A world in which gender inequality had been ended would be equally radical – revolutionary or reformist if you like. Not only on traditional criteria are gender inequalities sustained worldwide, but they are, in some respects, being accentuated by the pressure of the market on everyday and interpersonal, as well as family, life and by the rise of communitarian movements, too easily indulged by critics of imperialism in the developed world. Those critics of Marxism who argue that socio-economic analysis cannot encompass the intimate and the interpersonal miss the degree to which these are invaded by market forces themselves. The class and gender effects of globalization are multiple, but include, in some areas, the rolling-back of workplace, and equality, principles, as well as the wave of misogynist propaganda, pornography and gendered stereotyping that globalization has stimulated. The transnationalism of labour includes an estimated 700,000 women a year forcibly removed from one country to another for sexual exploitation. The fallacy of the revolutionary critique is, therefore, a twofold one: an overstatement not only of the possibility, but the very import of revolution, and a denial of the long-term, radical, transformative and constantly renewable potential of such a programme.

The Claims of Community

Any argument in favour of an approach based on principles such as these three will, inevitably, encounter the objection that concepts of rights, and therefore political values in general, vary as between peoples, and are, because these concepts assume universalism, invalid. Chapter 8 has already considered the ways in which culture is used within contemporary political discourse. Culture is equally at the centre of ethical debate, in opposition to universal claims in favour of claims made in culture's name. Here community, or nation, claims primacy as against broader, internationally pertinent, values and political pressures. The contemporary world offers a growing divergence between two forms of discourse – a universalist discourse with regard to rights, as embodied in international conventions, and a discourse that denies such universality, on the grounds of community, identity and, in the international sphere, sovereignty. Three different strands have contributed to this questioning of universality: an anti-imperialist critique of western domination and double standards; a post-modernist denial of the possibility of fixed, rational criteria for judgement; and a questioning within political theory of the bases of rights, a critique related to the broader questioning of Enlightenment and legal rationality.

We do not have to look far to see the implications of this critique: in international relations this takes the form of attacks by such states as China, Iran or Russia on western, or UN, criticism of human rights policies, as in US, British or Japanese resentment at the questioning of their legal and social practices; in communal relations within societies we see resistance to legal and ethical universalism by those who speak for, or claim to speak for, communities. As already suggested there is a factual, representational question here: when states claim to speak in the name of cultural exceptionalism against human rights, an equal scepticism should be in order. But even if this is so, the traditional, the inherited, can be balanced against other criteria, and for several reasons. One is in the legal sense positive: if states have signed up to international bodies and legal codes, they can, and should, be held accountable to them. This goes not only for the various UN Codes specifically concerned with political and social rights, but also for the Charter itself. All 189 countries in the world, whatever their cultural or religious heritage, that are signatories of the Charter are committed by dint of that very document to respect for basic human rights, as well as to basic norms of international behaviour: the Preamble, and Articles 1, 13 and 55 of the Charter commit the signatory states to opposing discrimination on the basis of race, religion or sex. More than half a century down the line, we can say that no state in the world has fully met this obligation.

A second reason for questioning the denial of universality, and in particular the ways in which political theorists seek to challenge rights, is to be found in the universalism implicit in the very language used by those who reject criticisms. There are, very obviously, certain moral claims which no state in the world, and no community either, questions: the right of nations to self-determination and the principle of sovereignty of states are two such universally espoused principles. No culture rejects the principle of self-determination, any more than any country wishes to be excluded from the World Cup. When we look in more detail at the criticisms made of rights in the international arena, underlying the criticisms is a logic that is also universalistic not particularistic. The charge of double standards implies, of necessity, that there are universal standards that should be, but are not being, respected. If Iraq denounces the west for double standards on

Palestine, or the Serbs denounce it for double standards on Kosovo, or the Turks raise the question of Chechnya, or if Arabs question western silence on Saudi Arabia, this is because these critics imply that universal standards are valid, and should be implemented.

If we look at the terms in which criticism of human rights is rejected, a similar universalism is to be identified. When China or Iran rejects western criticism, it is not mainly in the name of tradition – Confucianism, or Shi'ite Islam. Criticism is rejected in the name of sovereignty, of the primacy of economic over political rights at various stages of development, and by questioning the motives, and consistency, of those doing the criticizing. Again, the debate is framed within a set of universal criteria to which all subscribe, not by reference to a different culture. Indeed, the best form of defence being attack, it is not surprising that these countries riposte by denouncing the west for *its* failure to meet universal criteria – by neglecting their elderly, discriminating against migrants, promoting pornography, or committing war crimes in Kosovo or Iraq. Differences there are, but the differences of emphasis and argument are expressed within a universal language.

A striking example of the appeal of universal principles comes from Iran. In early 2000, London played host to a visit from the foreign minister of the Islamic Republic of Iran, Dr Kamal Kharrazi, the first official visit by an Iranian minister to London since the revolution of 1979. Speaking at the Royal Institute of International Affairs, Dr Kharrazi began by asserting that, indeed, the world was divided by culture: but he then went on to specify what he meant, that there were two cultures 'the culture of exclusion' and 'the culture of inclusion'. The culture of exclusion was marked by centralization, authoritarianism and the evasion of law, discrimination and injustice, accumulation of wealth and militarism. That of inclusion was marked by cultural pluralism and diversity, democracy, freedom, participation, justice, tolerance and collective security. 'The culture of inclusion', he asserted, 'is the culture of free-minded, justice-seeking and peaceful persons. The new world order must be based on the principle of inclusion so that our world will manage to pass through the remaining traces of the culture of obscurantism and move towards the culture of a new enlightenment, and put our global house in order on the basis of the rule of law and equity.' He quoted John Locke as well as Iranian President Khatami. He endorsed a range of contemporary political goals – civil society, human rights, good governance, confidence building. He recognized a diversity of human rules and religions. There was one reference to Islam, in his call for the need to promote 'good governance on the basis of Islamic teachings'. This was a voice that was critical of the west, and based on a particular reading of Islamic and Iranian values, but was, at the same time, part of a broader, global, anti-hegemonic and human vision. There was little to comfort the cultural relativists, or Samuel Huntington, in what he said.

The claims of community can also be held to account against the criteria of international and domestic peace themselves, in regard above all to inter-communal conflict. Here we see claims about territory, boundaries, holy places, historic sites, place and street names held up as if they were somehow to be respected, or accommodated. From the Garvaghy Road in Northern Ireland, through Kosovo Field, Nazareth and Jerusalem, to Ayodhya in India this pattern of historical legitimation about place is used to promote claim and conflict. The efforts of well-intentioned mediators go into trying to find an accommodation, recognition or respect for the various sensibilities and traditions involved. But maybe this is to concede too much. It may be suggested that such claims, far from acquiring greater legitimacy the longer they go back in time, have a receding, discounted validity the further they rest on history. If people have worshipped, chanted, marched or done whatever they do for centuries, that should perhaps be sufficient. The problem in Northern Ireland is not two conflicting traditions, it is tradition itself. The problem in Jerusalem is not the lack of respect for the three religions, it is too much respect for all of them and their sanctimonious claims: indeed the Crimean War began over a dispute in 1854 between different Christian claimants to the guardianship of the holy places in Jerusalem. A dispute over the administration of the multi-faith and multi-ethnic city of Jerusalem was long one of the major obstacles to a resolution of the Arab-Israeli dispute, a grotesque hostage-taking of the lives of millions of people by cultural manipulation. What does it matter which holy person of centuries ago was or was not buried in Ayodhya, when the cost of disputing this leads to the loss of lives and continuing inter-communal tensions? A bit of modernist impatience and scepticism about both the truth and ethical validity of communal claims would not be out of order today. In some cases the 'understanding' which the outside world accords such special pleading may be misplaced.

Universalism Imperilled

It is not possible to leave this issue without passing some comment on the manner in which these questions are discussed within western academic circles, and in the broad communitarian and other liberal abandonments of universalism. The arguments on which this approach are made are, in their own terms, questionable. Too much credence is given to the autonomy and validity of 'communities', itself a suspect word. Too much unqualified reverence is shown to tradition: here false history and bad sociology combine with a loss of ethical nerve.

The claim that the past conveys legitimacy on the present, for individuals and communities, would have shocked our liberal, and Enlightenment, predecessors. For them, and for all those who over the past century or more have striven for modernity in traditional society, the past was something certainly to be questioned, probably, indeed presumptively, to be rejected, a shackle to be cast off, a drag on our progress towards a better world. Heritage was to be denounced, tradition defied. Those in Europe who renounced the church, those in the Jewish tradition who cast off the world of *shtetl* and the rabbi, those in India who rejected the claims of Hindu Brahmins, those in China who denounced footbinding, those in the Islamic world who called for the freeing of women from veiling and inequality, or wrote critical, textual and historical, analyses of the Koran all espoused such a modernist view. Today, we seem to have turned almost full circle, where all that is in the past is accepted. Quite apart from the question of who defines what the tradition is, this authority of tradition is a debatable assumption, for individuals and communities alike. The right of individuals to question their tradition, and community, must be recognized and must be linked, as it too rarely is, to a recognition that what are presented as homogeneous or consensual communities rarely are.

The dangers of capitulation to tradition are not hard to see. One striking example is in regard to women. All religions set out to define the appropriate role for women, and to subject them to forms of control – in regard to their place within the religion, in dress and in some religions also with regard to personal hygiene. Hinduism, which has lagged behind the monotheistic religions in formal discrimination against women, is now trying to subordinate women more systematically. Where religion claims such authority, the argument becomes entrapped: it turns on various interpretations of the tradition, the text, the examples of earlier, sanctified times. But this is not the point. Whatever the tradition says should be open to question, on contemporary, critical, liberal and rights-based grounds. It may well be the case that in the past Chinese women had their feet bound, or Hindu women were burnt when their husbands died, or Muslim women were genitally mutilated – even if they were, there is an argument against their being so treated today. All orthodox religions, indeed all deities known to man, are in violation of UN human rights conventions.

This respect for community combines with a broader scepticism, evident on the left and right, about the possibility of defining, let alone implementing, universal norms. From several quarters we have heard that the west cannot solve all the problems of the world: here the kind of modish primordialism of a Robert Kaplan combines with the abstentionism of a John Rawls or a Gore Vidal. The London *Independent*[8] asked what right Hillary Clinton had to speak at the Beijing women's conference in 1995 on women's rights in the Third World, despite the fact that NGOs representing women from many Third World countries were at Beijing trying to break the monopoly of their own official representatives. Yet if instead of floundering in what is a self-enclosed western political space, these critics engaged on the ground, through visiting countries where the more extreme violations recurred or through reading the publications of Amnesty International or Human Rights Watch, they might have a different view of these matters. Enlightenment rationalism may look a bit tired from the metropolitan vantage point: it looks very different if you are being tortured or beaten in a jail, or if your male relatives are forcing you to submit to their will, or denying you an education.

Far more effective, and less easy to resolve in theory or practice, is the critique of anti-imperialism: this argues that the discourse of rights and the responsibility for their current implementation are wholly or largely in the hands of those states which, more than any others, have power in the contemporary world. These are also the states which have, over recent centuries, done more than any others to subjugate, exploit and control the rest of the world. This is a powerful charge, and one that is easily available to those who, without any commitment to rights or freedoms of any kind, wish to resist outside pressures. It is not, however, an insuperable one. Most law and most democratic institutions were initially forged by those with power: the question is whether they can over time, through democratic appropriation, be turned to more egalitarian use by those excluded from power. In international relations, this entails a recognition of the history of aggression of the powerful states and attention to overcoming the biases involved in such an origin: if the case for democratic appropriation applies within states, it may apply to relations between them. The argument for universal rights is not that we live in a perfect world, but that we live in one in which we face two broad kinds of choice – the abandonment of universal rights, for all their theoretical and practical drawbacks, and with that a possible descent into greater barbarity, or the search to turn the universality of principle into a universality of practice, while continuing to be sceptical of definition and implementation. There can be little doubt as to which the majority of humanity would prefer.

There is a need to be sceptical, and a little anxious, about the contemporary denial of universalism. The very celebration of community, when associated with claims of legitimacy for such communities and for the authority of those who happen to be controlling them, has in itself ethical and political dangers. Diversity of cultures can, and is, too easily allowed to involve a surrender of democratic control and individual rights. The abandonment in anti-rationalist and anti-foundationalist critique of the belief in any universal standards runs the risk of a return to a more brutal, chaotic world. As Jürgen Habermas has put it: 'The radical critique of reason exacts a high price for taking leave of modernity.'[9] Ask anyone who has been on the receiving end of violations of the Geneva Conventions in Chechnya, or Kosovo, or has been in a Taliban or *pasdaran* jail, if they think rights are part of a hegemonic project, and they will give you a sceptical look. They want *more* not *less* respect for universal norms.

The obstacles to making a rights argument come, however, not only from states but also from peoples. For many, indeed most, people in the world the use of a language of rights, with its universal basis, is combined with a strong sense of the entitlements of their own people, and the refusal to accord, in full or part, the same rights to others. We live in a world of outrage and claim, where the particular has a supreme authority that sweeps all before it. Western leaders may call on the peoples of former Yugoslavia to work together, but these appeals fall on largely deaf ears. A US president may appeal to India and Pakistan to settle their differences, but they have shown scant interest in so doing. In Northern Ireland, by comparison a very low-level, contained conflict, it has taken years of negotiation and patient engagement to get the parties to envisage a compromise, and it may take more years to reach a stable resolution. Too often minor, or symbolic, issues are used to imperil the welfare of many. The twentieth century would have done well to retain Lenin's category of 'nationalist bickering'.

The challenge is not to deny the importance of culture. In the areas where diversity and creativity prevail, this is one of the great sources of richness for all of humanity and it will continue to be so. One aspect of the modernist progressivist vision that we should be happy to see the back of is that of a world in which we are all the same, and speak one language. Modernity is more than compatible with diversity. Yet this diversity in language, religion, dress, music does not entail political conflict or the rejection of universal values on political issues. The dangers of that are evident in the reassertion of traditional, that is, undemocratic, forms of authority in communities, in the fostering of inter-communal conflict within states, and in the promotion of international conflict.

Beyond all of these debates lies one of the greatest dangers of modernity, and of the transnational world we inhabit, namely a narrowing of horizons in much of the developed world: the declining coverage of international news in press and media, and the spurious pursuit of 'family viewing' and other forms of intellectual capitulation are undermining not only the possibility of intelligent, measured discussion of these issues but also of concerted internationalist action by states, NGOs or individuals. The first precondition for humanitarian action, or human rights, is an informed internationalist discussion, something to which the press and media in the developed countries have less and less commitment. It is one of the paradoxes of this increasingly globalized, and transnational, world that the increasing integration of the globe should be accompanied by a narrowing of concern, analytic and ethical, on the part of many in the developed world. This is a trend which, while celebrating the diversity of world cultures, and appearing to pay respect to other people, tends more and more to abandon concern for them. This is, as much as anything, one of the moral challenges facing the world, and in particular the system of global governance, at the start of this new millennium.

Agency in Our Time

It is against this background, that it becomes possible to look at the world of this new millennium, and at the processes which may shape the world of the coming decades. To do this is a rash, some would say foolish, venture. Yet it merits an attempt, if only to identify those areas over which some degree of human control, be it individual, global, or vested in particular states, can be exercised. Indeed the single most important lesson of history, of the twentieth or any other century, has to be the need to keep in sight the possibilities for conscious human action, for agency, and, in our own times, for agency mediated through democratic states. To overstate this is to fall into a voluntarist folly, of believing that all suffering, death, war, or misunderstanding can be abolished. Agency evades easy definition or identification. Behind much of the more visionary writing on politics and on international relations there lies a rather vague concept of agency, remotely derived from Marxism but without a specific identification of the working class as the prime mover: instead a broader category of social movements or 'emancipatory' subjects' is invoked. At its more authoritarian margins, much in evidence in the twentieth century, this involves believing in the possibility of imposing a set of idealized plans on humanity or a particular country: progress, interpreted by an elite, will solve all. This was, in variant forms, the illusion, murderous when confounded, of both European colonialism and of authoritarian socialism.

Yet the alternative is morally even more reprehensible, involving a denial of what humans can and do achieve, and a transfer of responsibility to impersonal forces. In the past, familiar displacements were on hand: God, or gods, fate, nature, the stars, or other supposed unchangeable determinants of human behaviour – climate, class, gender, race. Today, the human will seems unstoppable, but there is a new atmosphere of determinist fatalism about, this time related to the three idealized forces, and it can be argued, fetishes, of the age – the market, the microchip and the genome.

The prominence of these three factors in discussion of the contemporary world highlights the most striking difference between the Zeitgeist of 1900 and that of 2000: where the former was expressive of a limitless, certainly overstated, belief in the possibility of human agency, above all collective human agency, to transform the world, the trademark of the latter is a more passive, deterministic faith in the beneficial potential of scientific and technological development. Much public discussion and not a little academic debate are shaped by recourse to these three fetishes, in some combination, as inevitable and therefore acceptable forces in human development. That all three themselves require mediation through human socialization and human will, that their outcomes in terms of individual behaviour, or the behaviour of groups, are variant seems easily forgotten. The market can enrich and impoverish, it can create or destroy. Some human products are suitable for marketization, others such as dignity, freedom, academic standards and privacy are arguably not, nor indeed is the environment. Information technology too has multiple effects – it can create greater individual freedom, it can strengthen states and fragment collective endeavour. It can promote greater equality between men and women, it can reinforce male privilege. The genome will, as its secrets are unveiled in what promises to be the century of biology, after those of chemistry and physics, tell us more about natural endowments, and, as it is mapped, enhance the medical prospects of millions. It will tell us rather less about human will, capability and creativity.

None of these discoveries will answer moral questions, and questions of choice, which lie at the basis of human freedom and democratic deliberation. That task depends on a democratic political order on the one hand, and the development of a critical international reason on the other. It is not history, or fate, or structures, or science that is going to shape the world at 2000: it is conscious, responsible, organized individuals. And we have to start by understanding how the world works and what we can do to influence it: that is the biggest challenge of all. The most important human activity, and also the precondition for wealth, is education. Schiller's epigram, in his *On the Aesthetic Education of Man*, that one is both a citizen of one's state and of one's age, was never more relevant than it is today.[10] That, in sum, is the challenge that the year 2000 has set for international reason.

Notes

1 A World in Transition

1. 'Peace impossible, war improbable'.
2. For a cogent alternative view, one that is sceptical of pessimism and more forthright in its belief in progress than the analysis here, see Barry Buzan and Gerald Segal, *Anticipating the Future: Twenty Millennia of Human Progress* (London: Simon & Schuster, 1997).
3. Eric Hobsbawm with Antonio Polito, *The New Century* (London: Little, Brown, 2000).
4. 'The Breaking of Nations – and the Threat to Ours', *The National Interest*, **26**, Winter 1991–92.
5. Paul Kennedy, *The Rise and Fall of the Great Powers: Economic Change and Military Conflict from 1500 to 2000* (London: HarperCollins, 1988).

2 The Shadow of the Twentieth Century

1. Eric Hobsbawm, *Age of Extremes. The Short Twentieth Century 1914 –1991* (London: Michael Joseph, 1994).
2. This summary draws heavily on those who have analysed the conflicts, and resolutions, of the twentieth century: Karl Polanyi, *The Great Transformation* (Boston: Beacon Press, 1957); Eric Hobsbawm, *Age of Extremes;* Gabriel Kolko, *Century of War* (New York: The New Press, 1994).
3. Quoted in Martin Jay, *The Dialectical Imagination* (London: Heinemann, 1973, p. 121).
4. Robin Blackburn, *The Making of New World Slavery* (London: Verso, 1997); Mark Cocker, *Rivers of Blood, Rivers of Gold: Europe's Conflict with Tribal Peoples* (London: Jonathan Cape, 1998); Lisa Potts, *The World Labour Market. A History of Migration* (London: Zed, 1990).
5. Francis Fukuyama, *The End of History and the Last Man* (London: Hamish Hamilton, 1992).
6. A point well made in Sami Zubaida on, 'Human Rights and Cultural Difference: Middle Eastern Perspectives', *New Perspectives on Turkey*, Fall 1994, no. 10.

3 Arguments about World Politics

1. Robert Kaplan, *The Ends of the Earth: A Journey at the Dawn of the 21st Century* (New York: Random House, 1996).
2. Zaki Laidi, *A World Without Meaning. The Crisis of Meaning in International Politics* (London: Routledge, 1998, pp. 1, 178).

3. Francis Fukuyama, *The End of History and the Last Man*, Chapter 2, note 5; Thomas Friedman, *The Lexus and the Olive Tree* (London: HarperCollins, 1999).

4. In 1995, in the course of a set of interviews with US foreign policy makers, I asked Dr Henry Kissinger, the former US secretary of state and author of books on the balance of power, what the role of the balance was in the post-cold-war world. His answer indicated that he, like the rest of us, did not have a clear view on this question: 'Very difficult, very complicated. I would answer that there are various kinds of balances of power that have to be dealt with simultaneously – economic, political, maybe military. I would really now no longer say balance of power as much as equilibrium. It's more or less the same thing, but not exactly the same thing. I would add to it an equilibrium between ends and means. It's the unanswered question of our period, for which America is very badly prepared.' Fred Halliday, *From Potsdam to Perestroika. Conversations with Cold Warriors* (London: BBC Publications, 1995, p. 33).

5. Robert Cooper, *The Post-modern State and World Order*, 2nd edn (London: Demos and the Foreign Policy Centre, 2000).

6. For one cautious variant, see John Ruggie, *Constructing the World Polity. Essays on International Institutionalization* (London: Routledge, 1998).

7. Quoted in Roy Denman, 'As Old Fault Line Becomes Clear, Some Will Proceed Alone', *International Herald Tribune*, 11 July 2000.

8. I am grateful to Mel James of Amnesty International for this.

9. A.J.P. Taylor, *The Troublemakers. Dissent over Foreign Policy 1792–1939* (Harmondsworth: Penguin, 1985).

10. For example, *Our Global Neighbourhood, the Report of the Commission on Global Governance* (Oxford: Oxford University Press, 1995, pp. 206–8).

11. E.H. Carr, *The Twenty Years' Crisis 1919–39* (London: Macmillan, 1983), Ch. 6, 'The Limitations of Realism'.

12. Mark Curtis, *The Great Deception. Anglo-American Power and World Order* (London: Pluto, 1998); Peter Gowan, *The Global Gamble. Washington's Faustian Bid for World Dominance* (London: Verso, 1999); Tariq Ali (ed.) *Masters of the Universe. NATO's Balkan Crusade* (London: Verso, 2000).

13. Noam Chomsky, *The New Military Humanism. Lessons from Kosovo.* (London: Pluto, 1999).

14. Edward Said, *Peace and its Discontents* (New York: Vintage, 1995).

15. Alain Minc, *Le Nouveau Moyen Age* (Paris: Gallimard, 1993); Robert Harvey, *The Return of the Strong: The Drift to Global Disaster* (London: Macmillan, 1995); Robert Kaplan, *To The Ends of the Earth*, see note 1. In separate vein, see Christopher Coker, *The Twilight of the West* (Oxford: Westview Press, 1998).

16. Peter Fleming, *Bayonets to Lhasa* (London: Rupert Hart-Davis, 1961, pp. 151–2).

4 The Recurrence of War

1. *Financial Times*, 26 November 1999.

2. I have gone into this in greater detail in 'Europe and the International System: War and Peace', in Stephen Chan and Jarrod Wiener (eds) *Twentieth Century International History* (London: I.B. Tauris, 1999).

3. Dan Smith, *The State of War and Peace Atlas*, 3rd edn (London: Penguin, 1997); *Strategic Survey, 1999/2000* (London: International Institute for Strategic Studies).

4. Mary Kaldor, *New and Old Wars: Organized Violence in the Global Era* (Cambridge: Polity Press, 1999); Michael Ignatieff, *The Warrior's Honour: Ethnic War and the Modern Conscience* (London: Chatto & Windus, 1998).

5. For a cogent critique from within the subcontinent, see Praful Bidwai and Achin Vanaik, *New Nukes: India, Pakistan and Global Disarmament* (Oxford: Signal Books, 2000).

6. Achin Vanaik, *The Furies of Indian Communalism: Religion, Modernity and Secularization* (London: Verso, 1997).

7. *Time*, 14 February 1983.

8. Lawrence Freedman, *The Revolution in Strategic Affairs* (London: International Institute for Strategic Studies, 1998).

5 Globalization and its Discontents

1. Amidst a vast literature I have drawn in particular on Paul Hirst and Graham Thompson, *Globalisation in Question, The International Economy and the Possibilities of Governance* (Cambridge: Polity Press, 1996); Paul Hirst, 'The Global Economy – Myths and Realities', *International Affairs* **73**(3) July 1997; Harry Gelber, *Sovereignty Through Interdependence* (London: Kluwer, 1997); David Held, Anthony McGrew, David Goldblatt and Jonathan Perraton, *Global Transformations* (Cambridge: Polity Press, 1999); Anthony Giddens, *Runaway World* (London: Profile Books, 1999); Jan Aart Scholte, *Globalization, A Critical Introduction* (London: Macmillan, 2000.)

2. UNDP *Human Development Report*, 1999, pp. 25–31.

3. UNDP 1999, p. 28.

4. The United Nations Conference on Trade and Development uses an 'index of transnationality' based on an average of ratios of foreign assets to total assets; foreign sales to total sales; foreign employment to total employment. McDonald's and Coca-Cola have low scores because of the large US market (*The Economist*, 27 September, 1990).

5. Paul Krugman, *The Return of Depression Economics* (London: Allen Lane, 1999).

6. The World Bank, *World Development Report 1999/2000* (Oxford: Oxford University Press, 1999, p. 9).

7. Robert Shiller, *Irrational Exuberance* (Princeton: Princeton University Press, 2000).

8. *International Herald Tribune*, January 2000.

9. *International Herald Tribune*, 20 April 2000.

10. Karl Polanyi, *The Great Transformation* (Boston: Beacon Press, 1957).

6 The Fragility of Democracy

1. 'Idea for a Universal History from a Cosmopolitan Point of View' (1784) ; 'Perpetual Peace' (1795), in Immanuel Kant, *On History*, edited by Lewis White Beck (New York: Bobbs-Merrill, 1963).
2. Samuel Huntington, *The Third World. Democratization in the Late Twentieth Century* (Norman: University of Oklahoma Press, 1993).
3. The works of Noberto Bobbio and of Jürgen Habermas are examples of such re-evaluation.
4. John Rawls, *The Law of Peoples* (Cambridge, MA: Harvard University Press, 1999).
5. Jack Snyder, *From Voting to Violence. Democratization and Nationalist Conflict* (London: W.W. Norton, 2000).
6. On this, see the classic article by Göran Therborn, 'The Rule of Capital and the Rise of Democracy' *New Left Review*, 103 May–June 1977.
7. On falling trust in political institutions and decline in political participation, Susan Pharr and Robert Putnam (eds) *Disaffected Democracies* (Princeton: Princeton University Press, 2000).
8. See note 5.
9. *International Herald Tribune*, 3 July 2000.
10. Robert Cooper, *The Postmodern State and World Order*, 2nd edn (London: Demos and the Foreign Policy Centre, 2000).

7 The Unaccountable Hegemon

1. *International Herald Tribune*, 18–19 January 1997.
2. Thomas Friedman, *The Lexus and the Olive Tree* (London: HarperCollins, 1999, p. 384).
3. Jean Baudrillard, *America* (New York: 1989), p. 77, quoted in Bruce Cumings, 'Still the American Century' in Michael Cox et al. (eds) *The Interregnum* (Cambridge: Cambridge University Press, 1999, p. 279).
4. Susan Strange, *Casino Capitalism* (Oxford: Blackwell, 1986); Michael Cox, *US Foreign Policy After the Cold War. Superpower without a Mission* (London: Pinter and Royal Institute of International Affairs, 1995).
5. See Ch. 1, note 5.
6. For example, Christopher Lasch, 'The Cold War Has Been Won at High Cost', *International Herald Tribune*, 13 July 1990.
7. Michael Klare, 'The Traders and the Prussians', *Seven Days* (New York), 28 March 1977, pp. 32–3.
8. For a moderate version of this argument, see Alan Wolfe, *The Rise and Fall of the Soviet 'Threat'* (Washington: Institute for Policy Studies, 1979); for my own critique, Fred Halliday, *The Making of the Second Cold War* (London: Verso, 1983).
9. *International Herald Tribune*, 1 March 1999. For a more robust case for multilateralism 'We are *not* the World. A New Vision for Foreign Policy', *The Nation* Special Issue, 8 May 2000.

8 Delusions of Difference

1. Samuel Huntington, *The Clash of Civilisations and the Remaking of World Order* (New York: Simon & Schuster, 1996, p. 108).
2. For a bracing critique of the 'Asian values' argument, see Michael Leifer, 'Tigers, Tigers Spurning Rights', *Times Higher Educational Supplement*, 21 April 1995.
3. Barrington Moore, *The Social Origins of Dictatorship and Democracy* (London: Allen Lane, 1967, p. 486).
4. Eric Hobsbawm and Terence Ranger (eds) *The Invention of Tradition* (Cambridge: Cambridge University Press, 1983).
5. Voltaire, *Lettres Philosophiques* (Paris: Garnier-Flammarion, 1964, p. 47, author's translation).

9 Governance Beyond Frontiers

1. Jacques Attali, *Dictionnaire du XXIe siècle* (Paris: Fayard, 1998, pp. 146–7).
2. I have developed this distinction in Fred Halliday, 'Three Concepts of Internationalism', *International Affairs,* Spring 1998.
3. Boutros Boutros-Ghali, *Unvanquished. A US–UN Saga* (London: I.B. Tauris, 1998).

10 For a Radical Universalism

1. François Furet, *Le passé d'une illusion* (Paris: Laffont, 1995).
2. Perry Anderson 'The End of History' in *A Zone of Engagement* (London: Verso, 1993).
3. See Ch. 3, note 11.
4. Zymunt Bauman, *Socialism: The Impossible Utopia* (London: Allen & Unwin, 1976).
5. W.G. Runciman, *The Social Animal* (London: HarperCollins, 1998), Ch. 9, 'Possible and Impossible Worlds'.
6. Universal Declaration of Human Rights, International Covenant on Civil and Political Rights, International Convention on Civil and Political Rights, Convention on the Elimination of All Forms of Racial Discrimination, Convention on the Elimination of All Forms of Discrimination Against Women, Convention on the Rights of the Child, Convention Against Torture.
7. Amartya Sen, *Development as Freedom* (New York: Knopf, 1999).
8. *Independent*, 10 August 1995.
9. Jürgen Habermas, *The Philosophical Discourse of Modernity* (Cambridge: Polity Press, 1997, p. 336).
10. Quoted in Walter Kaufman, *Hegel* (London: Weidenfeld & Nicolson, 1965, p. 48).

Index